Learning NumPy Array

Supercharge your scientific Python computations by understanding how to use the NumPy library effectively

Ivan Idris

[PACKT] open source*
PUBLISHING   community experience distilled

BIRMINGHAM - MUMBAI

Learning NumPy Array

Copyright © 2014 Packt Publishing

All rights reserved. No part of this book may be reproduced, stored in a retrieval system, or transmitted in any form or by any means, without the prior written permission of the publisher, except in the case of brief quotations embedded in critical articles or reviews.

Every effort has been made in the preparation of this book to ensure the accuracy of the information presented. However, the information contained in this book is sold without warranty, either express or implied. Neither the author, nor Packt Publishing, and its dealers and distributors will be held liable for any damages caused or alleged to be caused directly or indirectly by this book.

Packt Publishing has endeavored to provide trademark information about all of the companies and products mentioned in this book by the appropriate use of capitals. However, Packt Publishing cannot guarantee the accuracy of this information.

First published: June 2014

Production Reference: 1060614

Published by Packt Publishing Ltd.
Livery Place
35 Livery Street
Birmingham B3 2PB, UK.

ISBN 978-1-78398-390-2

www.packtpub.com

Cover Image by Duraid Fatouhi (duraidfatouhi@yahoo.com)

Credits

Author
Ivan Idris

Reviewers
Jonathan Bright
Jaidev Deshpande
Mark Livingstone
Miklós Prisznyák

Commissioning Editor
Kartikey Pandey

Acquisition Editor
Mohammad Rizvi

Content Development Editor
Akshay Nair

Technical Editors
Shubhangi H. Dhamgaye
Shweta S. Pant

Copy Editor
Sarang Chari

Project Coordinator
Lima Danti

Proofreaders
Maria Gould
Kevin McGowen

Indexer
Hemangini Bari

Production Coordinator
Arvindkumar Gupta

Cover Work
Arvindkumar Gupta

About the Author

Ivan Idris has an MSc in Experimental Physics. His graduation thesis had a strong emphasis on applied computer science. After graduating, he worked for several companies as a Java developer, data warehouse developer, and QA analyst. His main professional interests are Business Intelligence, Big Data, and Cloud Computing. He enjoys writing clean, testable code and interesting technical articles. He is the author of *NumPy 1.5 Beginner's Guide* and *NumPy Cookbook*, *Packt Publishing*. You can find more information and a blog with a few NumPy examples at `ivanidris.net`.

> I would like to take this opportunity to thank the reviewers and the team at Packt Publishing for making this book possible. Also, I would like to thank my teachers, professors, and colleagues who taught me about science and programming. Last, but not least, I would like to acknowledge my parents, family, and friends for their support.

About the Reviewers

Jonathan Bright has a BS in Electrical Engineering from Rensselaer Polytechnic Institute, and specializes in audio electronics and digital signal processing. He's been programming in Python since import antigravity (the XKCD comic mentioning Python) and contributes to the NumPy and SciPy projects.

Jaidev Deshpande is a software developer at Enthought, Inc., working on software for data analysis and visualization. He's been a research assistant at the University of Pune and Tata Institute of Fundamental Research, working on signal processing and machine learning. He has worked on *Numpy Cookbook*, *Ivan Idris, Packt Publishing*.

Mark Livingstone started his career working for many years for three international computer companies (which no longer exist) in engineering/support/programming/training roles but got tired of being made redundant. He then graduated from Griffith University, Gold Coast, Australia, with a bachelor's degree in Information Technology in 2011. In 2013, he graduated with an honors in B.InfoTech and is currently pursuing his PhD. All his research software is written in Python on a Mac.

Mark enjoys mentoring students with special needs. He is a past chairperson of the IEEE Griffith University Gold Coast Student Branch, volunteers as a qualified Justice of the Peace at the local district courthouse and has been a Credit Union Director. He has also completed 104 blood donations.

In his spare time, he co-develops the Salstat2 statistics package available at `https://sourceforge.net/projects/s2statistical/`, which is multiplatform and uses wxPython, NumPy, SciPy, Scikit, Matplotlib, and a number of other Python modules.

Miklós Prisznyák is a senior software engineer with a scientific background. He graduated as a physicist from the Eötvös Lóránd University, the largest and oldest university in Hungary. He did his MSc thesis on Monte Carlo simulations of non-Abelian lattice quantum field theories in 1992. Having worked for three years in the Central Research Institute for Physics of Hungary, he joined MultiRáció Kft. in Budapest, a company founded by physicists, which specializes in mathematical data analysis and forecasting economic data.

His main project was the Small Area Unemployment Statistics System, which has been in official use at the Hungarian Public Employment Service since then. He learned about the Python programming language there in 2000. He set up his own consulting company in 2002 and then worked on various projects for insurance, pharmacy, and e-commerce companies, using Python whenever he could. He also worked in a European Union research institute in Italy, testing and enhancing a distributed, Python-based Zope/Plone web application.

He moved to Great Britain in 2007 and first worked with a Scottish start-up, using Twisted Python. Then he worked in the aerospace industry in England using, among other things, the PyQt windowing toolkit, the Enthought application framework, and the NumPy and SciPy libraries. He returned to Hungary in 2012 and rejoined MultiRáció, where he's been working on a Python extension module for OpenOffice/EuroOffice, using NumPy and SciPy again, which allows users to solve nonlinear and stochastic optimization and statistical problems.

Miklós likes to travel, read, and he is interested in science, linguistics, history, politics, the board game of Go, and quite a few other topics. Besides these, he always enjoys a good cup of coffee. However, spending time with his brilliant 11-year-old son, Zsombor, is the most important thing for him.

www.PacktPub.com

Support files, eBooks, discount offers, and more

You might want to visit `www.PacktPub.com` for support files and downloads related to your book.

Did you know that Packt offers eBook versions of every book published, with PDF and ePub files available? You can upgrade to the eBook version at `www.PacktPub.com` and as a print book customer, you are entitled to a discount on the eBook copy. Get in touch with us at `service@packtpub.com` for more details.

At `www.PacktPub.com`, you can also read a collection of free technical articles, sign up for a range of free newsletters and receive exclusive discounts and offers on Packt books and eBooks.

PACKTLiB

`http://PacktLib.PacktPub.com`

Do you need instant solutions to your IT questions? PacktLib is Packt's online digital book library. Here, you can access, read and search across Packt's entire library of books.

Why subscribe?

- Fully searchable across every book published by Packt
- Copy and paste, print and bookmark content
- On demand and accessible via web browser

Free access for Packt account holders

If you have an account with Packt at `www.PacktPub.com`, you can use this to access PacktLib today and view nine entirely free books. Simply use your login credentials for immediate access.

*I would like to dedicate this book to the memory of my late uncle, Sahid.
He will be missed.*

– Ivan Idris

Table of Contents

Preface	**1**
Chapter 1: Getting Started with NumPy	**7**
Python	**7**
Installing NumPy, Matplotlib, SciPy, and IPython on Windows	**8**
Installing NumPy, Matplotlib, SciPy, and IPython on Linux	**10**
Installing NumPy, Matplotlib, and SciPy on Mac OS X	**11**
Building from source	**14**
NumPy arrays	**14**
Adding arrays	15
Online resources and help	**18**
Summary	**18**
Chapter 2: NumPy Basics	**19**
The NumPy array object	**19**
The advantages of using NumPy arrays	20
Creating a multidimensional array	**21**
Selecting array elements	**21**
NumPy numerical types	**22**
Data type objects	24
Character codes	24
dtype constructors	25
dtype attributes	26
Creating a record data type	**26**
One-dimensional slicing and indexing	**27**
Manipulating array shapes	**28**
Stacking arrays	29
Splitting arrays	33
Array attributes	35
Converting arrays	38

Creating views and copies	39
Fancy indexing	40
Indexing with a list of locations	42
Indexing arrays with Booleans	43
Stride tricks for Sudoku	45
Broadcasting arrays	47
Summary	49
Chapter 3: Basic Data Analysis with NumPy	**51**
Introducing the dataset	51
Determining the daily temperature range	53
Looking for evidence of global warming	55
Comparing solar radiation versus temperature	57
Analyzing wind direction	61
Analyzing wind speed	62
Analyzing precipitation and sunshine duration	63
Analyzing monthly precipitation in De Bilt	66
Analyzing atmospheric pressure in De Bilt	67
Analyzing atmospheric humidity in De Bilt	69
Summary	71
Chapter 4: Simple Predictive Analytics with NumPy	**73**
Examining autocorrelation of average temperature with pandas	73
Describing data with pandas DataFrames	76
Correlating weather and stocks with pandas	78
Predicting temperature	79
Autoregressive model with lag 1	79
Autoregressive model with lag 2	80
Analyzing intra-year daily average temperatures	81
Introducing the day-of-the-year temperature model	83
Modeling temperature with the SciPy leastsq function	84
Day-of-year temperature take two	85
Moving-average temperature model with lag 1	87
The Autoregressive Moving Average temperature model	88
The time-dependent temperature mean adjusted autoregressive model	89
Outliers analysis of average De Bilt temperature	92
Using more robust statistics	94
Summary	95

Chapter 5: Signal Processing Techniques — 97
- Introducing the Sunspot data — 97
  - Sifting continued — 99
- Moving averages — 101
- Smoothing functions — 103
- Forecasting with an ARMA model — 105
- Filtering a signal — 107
  - Designing the filter — 108
- Demonstrating cointegration — 109
- Summary — 112

Chapter 6: Profiling, Debugging, and Testing — 113
- Assert functions — 114
  - The assert_almost_equal function — 114
  - Approximately equal arrays — 115
  - The assert_array_almost_equal function — 116
- Profiling a program with IPython — 117
- Debugging with IPython — 119
- Performing Unit tests — 122
- Nose tests decorators — 125
- Summary — 128

Chapter 7: The Scientific Python Ecosystem — 129
- Numerical integration — 129
- Interpolation — 130
- Using Cython with NumPy — 132
- Clustering stocks with scikit-learn — 134
- Detecting corners — 137
- Comparing NumPy to Blaze — 139
- Summary — 140

Index — 141

Preface

Congratulations on purchasing *Learning NumPy Array*! This was a smart investment, which is guaranteed to save you a lot of time Googling and searching through (online) documentation. You will learn all the essential things needed to become a confident NumPy user. NumPy started originally as part of SciPy and then was singled out as a fundamental library, which other open source Python APIs build on. As such, it is a crucial part of the common Python stack used for numerical and data analysis.

NumPy code is much cleaner than "straight" Python code that tries to accomplish the same task. There are fewer loops required, because operations work directly on arrays and matrices. The many conveniences and mathematical functions make life easier as well. The underlying algorithms have stood the test of time and have been designed with high performance in mind.

NumPy's arrays are stored more efficiently than in an equivalent data structure in base Python, such as in a list of lists. Array IO is significantly faster too. The performance improvement scales with the number of elements of an array. For large arrays, it really pays off to use NumPy. Files as large as several terabytes can be memory-mapped to arrays leading to optimal reading and writing of data. The drawback of NumPy arrays is that they are more specialized than plain lists. Outside of the context of numerical computations, NumPy arrays are less useful.

Large portions of NumPy are written in C. That makes NumPy faster than pure Python code. Finally, since NumPy is open source, you get all of the related advantages. The price is the lowest possible—free as in beer. You don't have to worry about licenses every time somebody joins your team or you need an upgrade of the software. The source code is available to everyone. This of course is beneficial to the code quality.

What this book covers

Chapter 1, Getting Started with NumPy, will guide you through the steps needed to install NumPy on your system and helps you create a basic NumPy application. We also successfully run a vector addition program.

Chapter 2, NumPy Basics, introduces you to NumPy arrays and fundamentals. In this chapter, we also learn that NumPy arrays can be sliced and indexed in an efficient manner. Here, we will understand the manipulation of shapes of various arrays.

Chapter 3, Basic Data Analysis with NumPy, tells us about learning data analysis with weather data analysis as an example. We will also explore the data from a KNMI weather station.

Chapter 4, Simple Predictive Analytics with NumPy, helps us attempt to predict the weather with simple models, such as Autoregressive Model with Lag 1 and Autoregressive Model with Lag 2.

Chapter 5, Signal Processing Techniques, gives us examples of signal processing and time series analysis. We look at smoothing with window functions and moving averages. We also touch upon the sifting process used by scientists to derive sunspot cycles. And we also get a demonstration of cointegration.

Chapter 6, Profiling, Debugging, and Testing, is about profiling, debugging, and testing, which are essential phases in the development cycle. We also cover unit testing, assert functions, and floating-point precision in depth.

Chapter 7, The Scientific Python Ecosystem, gives an overview of the Python ecosystem in which NumPy takes a central role. We also examine Cython, which is a relatively young programming language based on Python. We also have a look at Clustering, a type of machine learning algorithm.

What you need for this book

To try out the code samples in this book, you will need a recent build of NumPy. This means that you will need to have one of the Python versions supported by NumPy as well. Some code samples make use of the Matplotlib for illustration purposes. Matplotlib is not strictly required to follow the examples, but it is recommended that you install it too.

Here is a list of software used to develop and test the code examples:

- Python 2.7
- Cython-0.17-py2.7-macosx-10.8-intel.egg

- ipython-2.0.0_dev-py2.7.egg
- matplotlib-1.4.x-py2.7-macosx-10.9-intel.egg
- numpy-1.9.0.dev_e886943-py2.7-macosx-10.9-intel.egg
- pandas-0.8.2.dev_f5a74d4_20120725-py2.7-macosx-10.8-x86_64.egg
- pip-1.4.1-py2.7.egg
- statsmodels-0.6.0-py2.7-macosx-10.9-intel.egg

Needless to say, you don't need to have exactly this software and these versions on your computer. Python and NumPy is the absolute minimum you will need.

Who this book is for

This book is for a scientist, engineer, programmer or an analyst looking for a high quality open source mathematical library. Knowledge of Python is assumed. Also, some affinity or at least interest in mathematics and statistics is required.

Conventions

In this book, you will find a number of styles of text that distinguish between different kinds of information. Here are some examples of these styles, and an explanation of their meaning.

Code words in text are shown as follows: "In this example, we chose `numpy-1.8.0-win32-superpack-python2.7.exe`."

A block of code is set as follows:

```
start = datetime.now()
c = pythonsum(size)
delta = datetime.now() - start
print "The last 2 elements of the sum", c[-2:]
print "PythonSum elapsed time in microseconds", delta.microseconds
```

Any command-line input or output is written as follows:

```
$ python vectorsum.py 4000
```

Preface

New terms and **important words** are shown in bold. Words that you see on the screen, in menus or dialog boxes for example, appear in the text like this: "Click on the **Continue** button."

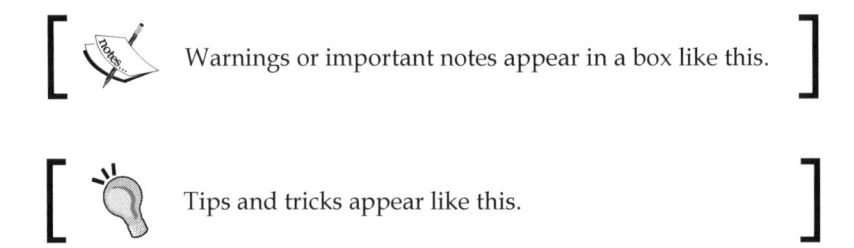

> Warnings or important notes appear in a box like this.

> Tips and tricks appear like this.

Reader feedback

Feedback from our readers is always welcome. Let us know what you think about this book—what you liked or may have disliked. Reader feedback is important for us to develop titles that you really get the most out of.

To send us general feedback, simply send an e-mail to feedback@packtpub.com, and mention the book title via the subject of your message.

If there is a topic that you have expertise in and you are interested in either writing or contributing to a book, see our author guide on www.packtpub.com/authors.

Customer support

Now that you are the proud owner of a Packt book, we have a number of things to help you to get the most from your purchase.

Downloading the example code

You can download the example code files for all Packt books you have purchased from your account at http://www.PacktPub.com. If you purchased this book elsewhere, you can visit http://www.PacktPub.com/support and register to have the files e-mailed directly to you.

Errata

Although we have taken every care to ensure the accuracy of our content, mistakes do happen. If you find a mistake in one of our books — maybe a mistake in the text or the code — we would be grateful if you would report this to us. By doing so, you can save other readers from frustration and help us improve subsequent versions of this book. If you find any errata, please report them by visiting http://www.packtpub.com/support, selecting your book, clicking on the **errata submission form** link, and entering the details of your errata. Once your errata are verified, your submission will be accepted and the errata will be uploaded on our website, or added to any list of existing errata, under the Errata section of that title. Any existing errata can be viewed by selecting your title from http://www.packtpub.com/support.

Piracy

Piracy of copyright material on the Internet is an ongoing problem across all media. At Packt, we take the protection of our copyright and licenses very seriously. If you come across any illegal copies of our works, in any form, on the Internet, please provide us with the location address or website name immediately so that we can pursue a remedy.

Please contact us at copyright@packtpub.com with a link to the suspected pirated material.

We appreciate your help in protecting our authors, and our ability to bring you valuable content.

Questions

You can contact us at questions@packtpub.com if you are having a problem with any aspect of the book, and we will do our best to address it.

Getting Started with NumPy

Let's get started. We will install NumPy and related software on different operating sytems and have a look at some simple code that uses NumPy. As mentioned in the *Preface*, SciPy is closely related to NumPy, so you will see the name SciPy appearing throughout the chapter. At the end of this chapter, you will find pointers on how to find additional information online if you get stuck or are uncertain about the best way to solve problems.

In this chapter, we shall learn the following skills:

- Installing Python, SciPy, Matplotlib, IPython, and NumPy on Windows, Linux, and Macintosh
- Writing simple NumPy code
- Adding arrays
- Making use of online resources and help

Python

NumPy is based on Python, so it is required to have Python installed. On some operating systems, Python is already installed. You, however, need to check whether the Python version is compatible with the NumPy version you want to install. There are many implementations of Python, including commercial implementations and distributions. In this book, we will focus on the standard CPython implementation, which is guaranteed to be compatible with NumPy.

NumPy has binary installers for Windows, various Linux distributions, and Mac OS X. There is also a source distribution, if you prefer that. You need to have Python 2.4.x or above installed on your system. Python 2.7.6 is currently the best Python version to have because most scientific Python libraries support it.

Installing NumPy, Matplotlib, SciPy, and IPython on Windows

Installing NumPy on Windows is a necessary but, fortunately, straightforward task that we will cover in detail. You only need to download an installer, and a wizard will guide you through the installation steps. It is recommended that Matplotlib, SciPy, and IPython be installed. However, this is not required to enjoy this book. The actions we will take are as follows:

1. Download a NumPy installer for Windows from the SourceForge website at `http://sourceforge.net/projects/numpy/files/`.

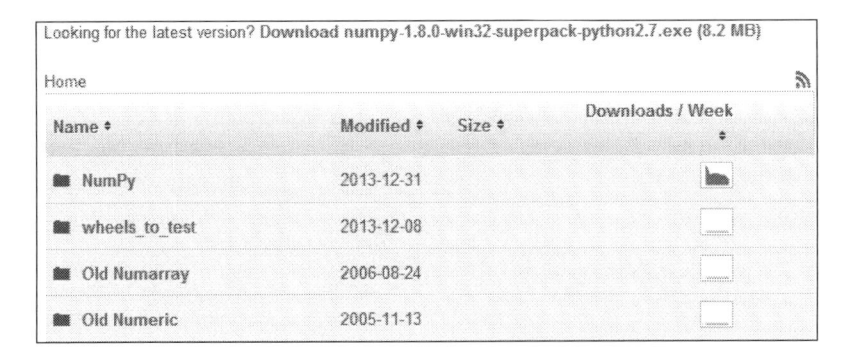

2. Choose the appropriate version. In this example, we chose `numpy-1.8.0-win32-superpack-python2.7.exe`.

3. Open the EXE installer by double-clicking on it.

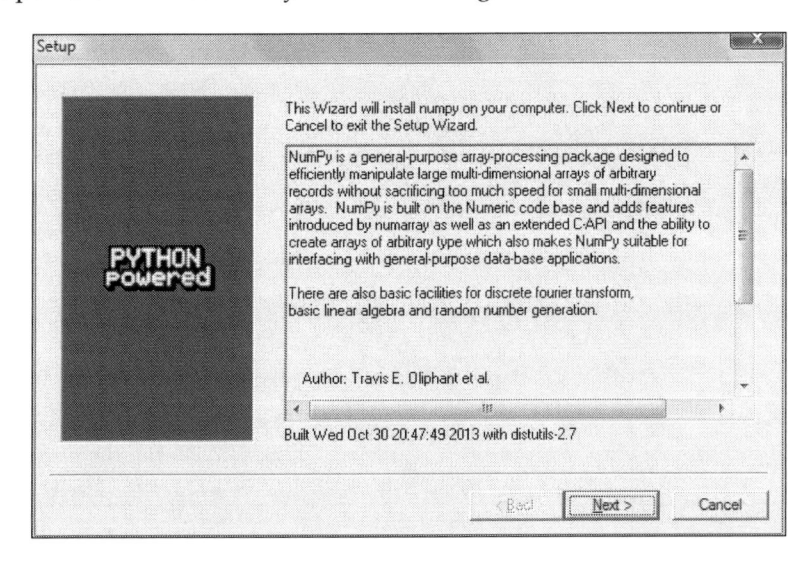

4. Now, we can see a description of NumPy and its features, as shown in the previous screenshot. Click on the **Next** button.

5. If you have Python installed, it should automatically be detected. If it is not detected, maybe your path settings are wrong. At the end of this chapter, resources are listed in case you have problems installing NumPy.

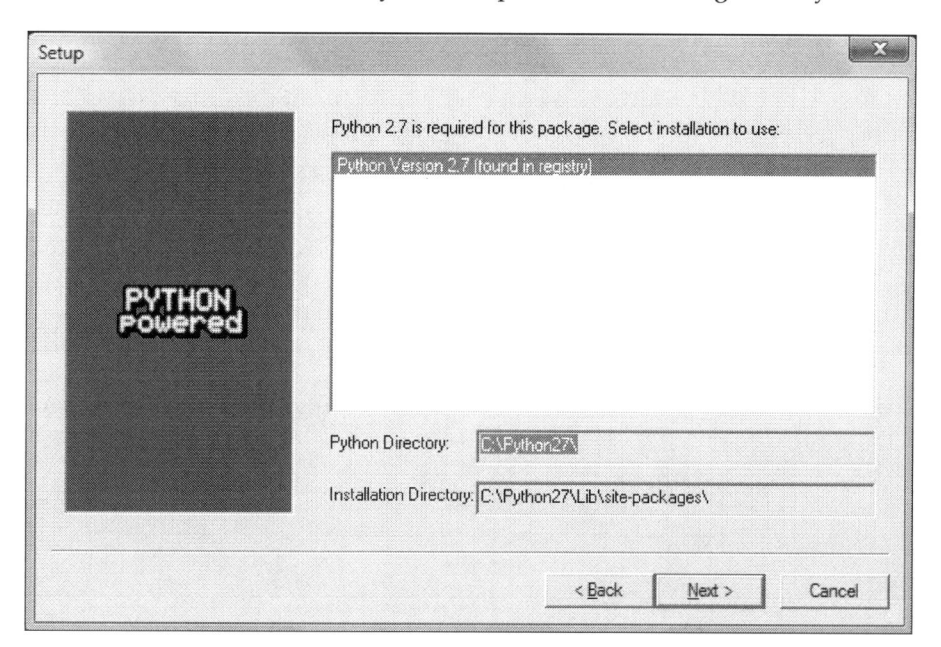

6. In this example, Python 2.7 was found. Click on the **Next** button if Python is found, otherwise, click on the **Cancel** button and install Python (NumPy cannot be installed without Python). Click on the **Next** button. This is the point of no return. Well, kind of, but it is best to make sure that you are installing to the proper directory and so on and so forth. Now the real installation starts. This may take a while.

7. Install SciPy and Matplotlib with the Enthought distribution at http://www.enthought.com/products/epd.php.

> The situation around installers is rapidly evolving. Other alternatives exist in various stage of maturity (see http://www.scipy.org/install.html). It might be necessary to put the msvcp71.dll file in your C:\Windows\system32 directory. You can get it at http://www.dll-files.com/dllindex/dll-files.shtml?msvcp71. A Windows IPython installer is available on the IPython website (see http://ipython.scipy.org/Wiki/IpythonOnWindows).

Installing NumPy, Matplotlib, SciPy, and IPython on Linux

Installing NumPy and related recommended software on Linux depends on the distribution you have. We will discuss how you would install NumPy from the command line although you could probably use graphical installers; it depends on your distribution (distro). The commands to install Matplotlib, SciPy, and IPython are the same—only the package names are different. Installing Matplotlib, SciPy, and IPython is recommended, but optional.

Most Linux distributions have NumPy packages. We will go through the necessary steps for some of the popular Linux distros:

- Run the following instructions from the command line for installing NumPy on Red Hat:

    `yum install python-numpy`

- To install NumPy on Mandriva, run the following command-line instruction:

    `urpmi python-numpy`

- To install NumPy on Gentoo, run the following command-line instruction:

    `sudo emerge numpy`

- To install NumPy on Debian or Ubuntu, we need to type the following:

    `sudo apt-get install python-numpy`

The following table gives an overview of the Linux distributions and corresponding package names for NumPy, SciPy, Matplotlib, and IPython:

Linux distribution	NumPy	SciPy	Matplotlib	IPython
Arch Linux	`python-numpy`	`python-scipy`	`python-matplotlib`	`ipython`
Debian	`python-numpy`	`python-scipy`	`python-matplotlib`	`ipython`
Fedora	`numpy`	`python-scipy`	`python-matplotlib`	`ipython`
Gentoo	`dev-python/numpy`	`scipy`	`matplotlib`	`ipython`
OpenSUSE	`python-numpy, python-numpy-devel`	`python-scipy`	`python-matplotlib`	`ipython`
Slackware	`numpy`	`scipy`	`matplotlib`	`ipython`

Installing NumPy, Matplotlib, and SciPy on Mac OS X

You can install NumPy, Matplotlib, and SciPy on the Mac with a graphical installer or from the command line with a port manager, such as MacPorts or Fink, depending on your preference.

> We can get a NumPy installer from the SourceForge website at `http://sourceforge.net/projects/numpy/files/`. Similar files exist for Matplotlib and SciPy. Just change `numpy` in the previous URL to `scipy` or `matplotlib`. IPython didn't have a GUI installer at the time of writing. Download the appropriate DMG file as shown in the following screenshot; usually the latest one is the best. Another alternative is the SciPy Superpack (`https://github.com/fonnesbeck/ScipySuperpack`). Whichever option you choose, it is important to make sure that updates which impact the system Python library don't negatively influence the already installed software by not building against the Python library provided by Apple.

Looking for the latest version? **Download numpy-1.8.0-py2.7-python.org-macosx10.6.dmg (11.0 MB)**

Home   f

Name	Modified	Size	Downloads / Week
o NumPy	2013-12-31		14,620 weekly downlo
o wheels_to_test	2013-12-08		9 weekly downloads
o Old Numarray	2006-08-24		12 weekly downloads
o Old Numeric	2005-11-13		68 weekly downloads

Getting Started with NumPy

We will install NumPy with a GUI installer using the following steps:

1. Open the DMG file as shown in the following screenshot (in this example, `numpy-1.8.0-py2.7-python.org-macosx10.6.dmg`):

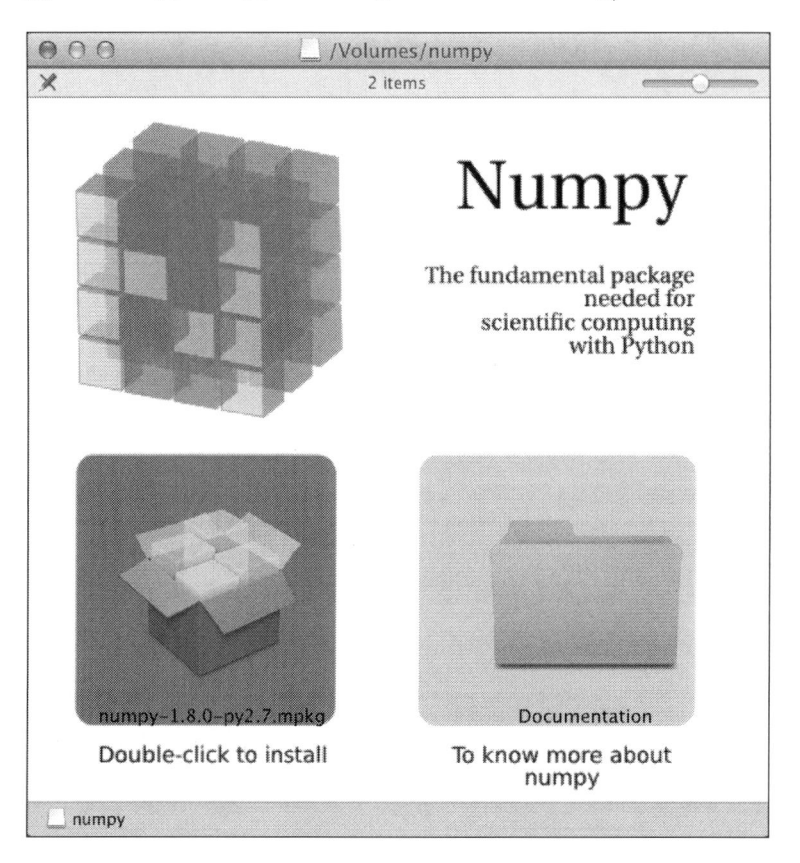

2. Double-click on the icon of the opened box, that is, the one having a subscript that ends with `.mpkg`. We will be presented with the welcome screen of the installer.

3. Click on the **Continue** button to go to the **Read Me** screen, where we will be presented with a short description of NumPy, as shown in the following screenshot:

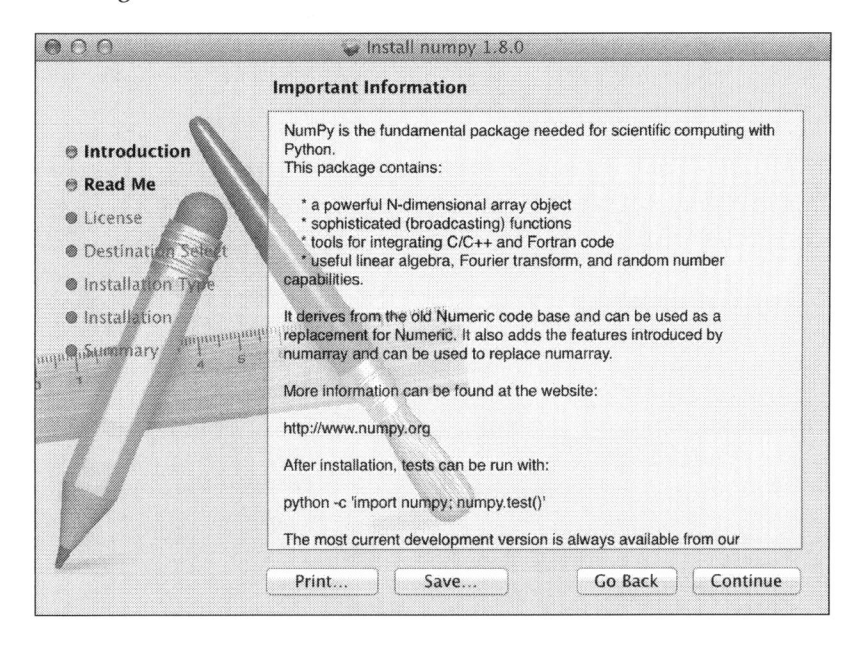

4. Click on the **Continue** button to go to the **License** screen.
5. Read the license, click on the **Continue** button, and then on the **Accept** button, when prompted to accept the license. Continue through the next screens and click on the **Finish** button at the end.

Alternatively, we can install NumPy, SciPy, Matplotlib, and IPython through the MacPorts route or with Fink. The following installation steps install all these packages. We only need NumPy for the tutorials in this book, so please omit the packages you are not interested in.

- To install with MacPorts, type the following command:

  ```
  sudo port install py-numpy py-scipy py-matplotlib py-ipython
  ```

- Fink also has packages for NumPy: `scipy-core-py24`, `scipy-core-py25`, and `scipy-core-py26`. The SciPy packages are: `scipy-py24`, `scipy-py25`, and `scipy-py26`. We can install NumPy and the other recommended packages that we will be using in this book for Python 2.6 with the following command:

  ```
  fink install scipy-core-py26 scipy-py26 matplotlib-py26
  ```

Building from source

As a last resort or if we want to have the latest code, we can build from source. In practice it shouldn't be that hard although, depending on your operating system, you might run into problems. As operating systems and related software are rapidly evolving, the best you can do is search online or ask for help. In this chapter, we give pointers on good places to look for help.

The steps to install NumPy from source are straightforward and given here. We can retrieve the source code for NumPy with `.git` as follows:

```
git clone git://github.com/numpy/numpy.git numpy
```

Install on `/usr/local` with the following command:

```
python setup.py build
sudo python setup.py install --prefix=/usr/local
```

To build, we need a C compiler such as GCC and the Python header files in the `python-dev` or `python-devel` package.

NumPy arrays

After going through the installation of NumPy, it's time to have a look at NumPy arrays. NumPy arrays are more efficient than Python lists when it comes to numerical operations. NumPy arrays are in fact specialized objects with extensive optimizations. NumPy code requires less explicit loops than the equivalent Python code. This is based on vectorization.

If we go back to high school mathematics, then we should remember the concepts of scalars and vectors. The number 2 for instance is a scalar. When we add 2 and 2, we are performing scalar addition. We can form a vector out of a group of scalars. In Python programming terms, we will then have a one-dimensional array. This concept can of course be extended to higher dimensions. Performing an operation on two arrays such as addition can be reduced to a group of scalar operations. In straight Python, we will do that with loops going through each element in the first array and adding it to the corresponding element in the second array. However, this is more verbose than the way it is done in mathematics. In mathematics, we treat the addition of two vectors as a single operation. That's the way NumPy arrays do it too and there are certain optimizations using low-level C routines, which make these basic operations more efficient. We will cover NumPy arrays in more detail in the next chapter.

Adding arrays

Imagine that we want to add two vectors called a and b. A vector is used here in the mathematical sense, which means a one-dimensional array. We will learn in *Chapter 4, Simple Predictive Analytics with NumPy,* about specialized NumPy arrays that represent matrices. The vector a holds the squares of integers 0 to n, for instance. If n is equal to 3, then a contains 0, 1, or 4. The vector b holds the cubes of integers 0 to n, so if n is equal to 3, then the vector b is equal to 0, 1, or 8. How would you do that using plain Python? After we come up with a solution, we will compare it with the NumPy equivalent.

The following function solves the vector addition problem using pure Python without NumPy:

```
def pythonsum(n):
    a = range(n)
    b = range(n)
    c = []

    for i in range(len(a)):
        a[i] = i ** 2
        b[i] = i ** 3
        c.append(a[i] + b[i])

    return c
```

The following is a function that achieves the same with NumPy:

```
def numpysum(n):
    a = numpy.arange(n) ** 2
    b = numpy.arange(n) ** 3
    c = a + b
    return c
```

Notice that numpysum() does not need a for loop. Also, we used the arange function from NumPy, which creates a NumPy array for us with integers 0 to n. The arange function was imported; that is why it is prefixed with numpy.

Now comes the fun part. Remember that it is mentioned in the *Preface* that NumPy is faster when it comes to array operations. How much faster is Numpy, though? The following program will show us by measuring the elapsed time in microseconds, for the numpysum and pythonsum functions. It also prints the last two elements of the vector sum. Let's check that we get the same answers when using Python and NumPy:

```
#!/usr/bin/env/python

import sys
```

Getting Started with NumPy

```
from datetime import datetime
import numpy as np

"""
 This program demonstrates vector addition the Python way.
 Run from the command line as follows

  python vectorsum.py n

 where n is an integer that specifies the size of the vectors.

 The first vector to be added contains the squares of 0 up to n.
 The second vector contains the cubes of 0 up to n.
 The program prints the last 2 elements of the sum and the elapsed time.
"""

def numpysum(n):
    a = np.arange(n) ** 2
    b = np.arange(n) ** 3
    c = a + b

    return c

def pythonsum(n):
    a = range(n)
    b = range(n)
    c = []

    for i in range(len(a)):
        a[i] = i ** 2
        b[i] = i ** 3
        c.append(a[i] + b[i])

    return c

size = int(sys.argv[1])

start = datetime.now()
c = pythonsum(size)
delta = datetime.now() - start
print "The last 2 elements of the sum", c[-2:]
```

```
    print "PythonSum elapsed time in microseconds", delta.microseconds

    start = datetime.now()
    c = numpysum(size)
    delta = datetime.now() - start
    print "The last 2 elements of the sum", c[-2:]
    print "NumPySum elapsed time in microseconds", delta.microseconds
```

The output of the program for the 1000, 2000, and 3000 vector elements is as follows:

```
$ python vectorsum.py 1000
The last 2 elements of the sum [995007996, 998001000]
PythonSum elapsed time in microseconds 707
The last 2 elements of the sum [995007996 998001000]
NumPySum elapsed time in microseconds 171
$ python vectorsum.py 2000
The last 2 elements of the sum [7980015996, 7992002000]
PythonSum elapsed time in microseconds 1420
The last 2 elements of the sum [7980015996 7992002000]
NumPySum elapsed time in microseconds 168
$ python vectorsum.py 4000
The last 2 elements of the sum [63920031996, 63968004000]
PythonSum elapsed time in microseconds 2829
The last 2 elements of the sum [63920031996 63968004000]
NumPySum elapsed time in microseconds 274
```

> **Downloading the example code**
>
> You can download the example code files for all Packt books you have purchased from your account at http://www.PacktPub.com. If you purchased this book elsewhere, you can visit http://www.PacktPub.com/support and register to have the files e-mailed directly to you.

Clearly, NumPy is much faster than the equivalent normal Python code. One thing is certain: we get the same results whether we are using NumPy or not. However, the result that is printed differs in representation. Notice that the result from the numpysum function does not have any commas. How come? Obviously we are not dealing with a Python list, but with a NumPy array. It was mentioned in the *Preface* that NumPy arrays are specialized data structures for numerical data. We will learn more about NumPy arrays in *Chapter 2, NumPy Basics*.

Online resources and help

The main documentation website for NumPy and SciPy is at `http://docs.scipy.org/doc/`. On this web page, we can browse the NumPy reference at `http://docs.scipy.org/doc/numpy/reference/` and the user guide, as well as several tutorials.

NumPy has a wiki with lots of documentation at `http://docs.scipy.org/numpy/Front%20Page/`.

The NumPy and SciPy forum can be found at `http://ask.scipy.org/en`.

The popular Stack Overflow software development forum has hundreds of questions tagged as `numpy`. To view them, go to `http://stackoverflow.com/questions/tagged/numpy`.

If you are really stuck with a problem or you want to be kept informed of NumPy's development, you can subscribe to the NumPy discussion mailing list. The e-mail address is `numpy-discussion@scipy.org`. The number of e-mails per day is not too high, and there is almost no spam to speak of. Most importantly, developers actively involved with NumPy also answer questions asked on the discussion group. The complete list can be found at `http://www.scipy.org/Mailing_Lists`.

For IRC users, there is an IRC channel on `irc://irc.freenode.net`. The channel is called `#scipy`, but you can also ask NumPy questions since SciPy users also have knowledge of NumPy, as SciPy is based on NumPy. There are at least 50 members on the SciPy channel at all times.

Summary

In this chapter, we installed NumPy and other recommended software that we will be using in some tutorials. We got a vector addition program working and convinced ourselves that NumPy has superior performance. In addition, we explored the available NumPy documentation and online resources.

In the next chapter, we will take a look under the hood and explore some fundamental concepts, including arrays and data types.

2
NumPy Basics

After installing NumPy and getting some code to work, it's time to cover NumPy basics. This chapter introduces you to the fundamentals of NumPy and arrays. At the end of this chapter you will have a basic understanding of NumPy arrays and their associated functions.

The topics that we shall cover in this chapter are as follows:

- Data types
- Array types
- Type conversions
- Creating arrays
- Indexing
- Fancy indexing
- Slicing
- Manipulating shapes

The NumPy array object

NumPy has a multidimensional array object called `ndarray`. It consists of two parts as follows:

- The actual data
- Some metadata describing the data

The majority of array operations leave the raw data untouched. The only aspect that changes is the metadata.

We have already learned in the previous chapter how to create an array using the `arange()` function. Actually, we created a one-dimensional array that contained a set of numbers. The `ndarray` object can have more than one dimension.

The advantages of using NumPy arrays

A NumPy array is a general homogeneous array—the items in an array have to be of the same type (there is a special array type that is heterogeneous). The advantage is that if we know that the items in an array are of the same type, it is easy to determine the storage size required for the array. NumPy arrays can perform vectorized operations working on a whole array. Contrast this to Python lists, where normally you have to loop through the list and perform operations on each element at a time. Also, NumPy uses an optimized C API for these operations, making them especially fast.

NumPy arrays are indexed just like in Python, starting from 0. Data types are represented by special objects. These objects will be discussed comprehensively further in this chapter.

We will create an array using the `arange()` function again (see the `arrayattributes.py` file in the `Chapter02` folder of this book's code bundle). In this chapter, you will see code snippets from IPython sessions where NumPy is already imported. The following code snippet shows us how to get the data type of an array:

```
In: a = arange(5)
In: a.dtype
Out: dtype('int64')
```

The data type of the array `a` is `int64` (at least on my machine), but you may get `int32` as the output if you are using 32-bit Python. In both cases, we are dealing with integers (64-bit or 32-bit). Apart from the data type of an array, it is important to know its shape. The example in *Chapter 1, Getting Started with NumPy*, demonstrated how to create a vector (actually, a one-dimensional NumPy array). A vector is commonly used in mathematics, but most of the time we need higher-dimensional objects. Let's determine the shape of the vector we created a little earlier in this section:

```
In: a
Out: array([0, 1, 2, 3, 4])
In: a.shape
Out: (5,)
```

As you can see, the vector has five elements with values ranging from `0` to `4`. The `shape` attribute of the array is a tuple; in this case, a tuple of one element, which contains the length in each dimension.

Creating a multidimensional array

Now that we know how to create a vector, we are ready to create a multidimensional NumPy array. After we create the matrix, we will again want to display its shape (see the `arrayattributes.py` file in the `Chapter02` folder of this book's code bundle), as shown in the following code snippets:

- To create a multidimensional array, see the following code:

    ```
    In: m = array([arange(2), arange(2)])
    In: m
    Out:
    array([[0, 1],
           [0, 1]])
    ```

- To display the array shape, see the following lines of code:

    ```
    In: m.shape
    Out: (2, 2)
    ```

We created a 2 x 2 array with the `arange()` function. Without any warning, the `array()` function appeared on the stage.

The `array()` function creates an array from an object that you give to it. The object needs to be array-like, for instance, a Python list. In the preceding example, we passed in a list of arrays. The object is the only required argument of the `array()` function. NumPy functions tend to have a lot of optional arguments with predefined defaults.

Selecting array elements

From time to time, we will want to select a particular element of an array. We will take a look at how to do this, but first, let's create a 2 x 2 matrix again (see the `elementselection.py` file in the `Chapter02` folder of this book's code bundle):

```
In: a = array([[1,2],[3,4]])
In: a
Out:
array([[1, 2],
       [3, 4]])
```

The matrix was created this time by passing a list of lists to the `array()` function. We will now select each item of the matrix one at a time, as shown in the following code snippet. Remember, the indices are numbered starting from 0.

```
In: a[0,0]
Out: 1
In: a[0,1]
```

[21]

```
Out: 2
In: a[1,0]
Out: 3
In: a[1,1]
Out: 4
```

As you can see, selecting elements of the array is pretty simple. For the array `a`, we just use the notation `a[m,n]`, where `m` and `n` are the indices of the item in the array.

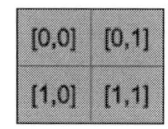

[0,0]	[0,1]
[1,0]	[1,1]

NumPy numerical types

Python has an integer type, a float type, and a complex type; however, this is not enough for scientific computing. In practice, we need even more data types with varying precision, and therefore, different memory size of the type. For this reason, NumPy has a lot more data types. The majority of NumPy numerical types end with a number. This number indicates the number of bits associated with the type. The following table (adapted from the NumPy user guide) gives an overview of NumPy numerical types:

Type	Description
bool	This stores boolean (True or False) as a bit
inti	This is a platform integer (normally either int32 or int64)
int8	This is an integer ranging from -128 to 127
int16	This is an integer ranging from -32768 to 32767
int32	This is an integer ranging from -2 ** 31 to 2 ** 31 -1
int64	This is an integer ranging from -2 ** 63 to 2 ** 63 -1
uint8	This is an unsigned integer ranging from 0 to 255
uint16	This is an unsigned integer ranging from 0 to 65535
uint32	This is an unsigned integer ranging from 0 to 2 ** 32 - 1
uint64	This is an unsigned integer ranging from 0 to 2 ** 64 - 1
float16	This is a half precision float with sign bit, 5 bits exponent, and 10 bits mantissa
float32	This is a single precision float with sign bit, 8 bits exponent, and 23 bits mantissa
float64 or float	This is a double precision float with sign bit, 11 bits exponent, and 52 bits mantissa

Type	Description
`complex64`	This is a complex number represented by two 32-bit floats (real and imaginary components)
`complex128` or `complex`	This is a complex number represented by two 64-bit floats (real and imaginary components)

For each data type, there exists a corresponding conversion function (see the numericaltypes.py file in the `Chapter02` folder of this book's code bundle), as shown in the following code snippet:

```
In: float64(42)
Out: 42.0
In: int8(42.0)
Out: 42
In: bool(42)
Out: True
In: bool(0)
Out: False
In: bool(42.0)
Out: True
In: float(True)
Out: 1.0
    In: float(False)
   Out: 0.0
```

Many functions have a data type argument, which is often optional:

```
In: arange(7, dtype=uint16)
Out: array([0, 1, 2, 3, 4, 5, 6], dtype=uint16)
```

It is important to know that you are not allowed to convert a complex number into an integer type number. Trying to do that triggers a `TypeError`, as shown in the following screenshot:

```
In [1]: int(42.0 + 1.j)
-----------------------------------------
TypeError
<ipython-input-1-5e824780381a> in <modu
----> 1 int(42.0 + 1.j)

TypeError: can't convert complex to int
```

The same goes for conversion of a complex number into a float type number. By the way, the **j** part is the imaginary coefficient of the complex number. However, you can convert a floating number to a complex number, for instance, `complex(1.0)`. The real and imaginary parts of a complex number can be extracted with the `real()` and `imag()` functions respectively.

Data type objects

Data type objects are instances of the `numpy.dtype` class. Once again, arrays have a data type. To be precise, every element in a NumPy array has the same data type. The data type object can tell you the size of the data in bytes. The size in bytes is given by the `itemsize` attribute of the `dtype` class (see the `dtypeattributes.py` file in the `Chapter02` folder of this book's code bundle), as shown in the following lines of code:

```
In: a.dtype.itemsize
Out: 8
```

Character codes

Character codes are included for backward compatibility with Numeric. Numeric is the predecessor of NumPy. Their use is not recommended, but the codes are provided here because they pop up in several places. You should instead use the `dtype` objects. The following table shows different data types and character codes associated with them:

Type	Character code
integer	i
Unsigned integer	u
Single precision float	f
Double precision float	d
bool	b
complex	D
string	S
unicode	U
Void	V

Look at the following code to create an array of single precision floats (see the charcodes.py file in the Chapter02 folder of this book's code bundle):

```
In: arange(7, dtype='f')
Out: array([ 0.,   1.,   2.,   3.,   4.,   5.,   6.], dtype=float32)
Likewise this creates an array of complex numbers
In: arange(7, dtype='D')
Out: array([ 0.+0.j,   1.+0.j,   2.+0.j,   3.+0.j,   4.+0.j,   5.+0.j,
    6.+0.j])
```

dtype constructors

We have a variety of ways to create data types. Take the case of floating point data (see the dtypeconstructors.py file in the Chapter02 folder of this book's code bundle) as follows:

- We can use the general Python float as shown in the following lines of code:
  ```
  In: dtype(float)
  Out: dtype('float64')
  ```

- We can specify a single precision float with a character code as shown in the following lines of code:
  ```
  In: dtype('f')
  Out: dtype('float32')
  ```

- We can use a double precision float character code as shown in the following lines of code:
  ```
  In: dtype('d')
  Out: dtype('float64')
  ```

- We can give a data type constructor a two-character code. The first character signifies the type, and the second character is a number specifying the number of bytes in the data type (the numbers 2, 4, and 8 correspond to 16-, 32-, and 64-bit floats, respectively), as shown in the following lines of code:
  ```
  In: dtype('f8')
  Out: dtype('float64')
  ```

A listing of all data type names can be found by calling sctypeDict.keys():

```
In: sctypeDict.keys()
Out: [0, …
 'i2',
 'int0']
```

dtype attributes

The `dtype` class has a number of useful attributes. For example, we can get information about the character code of a data type through the attributes of `dtype` (see the `dtypeattributes2.py` file in the `Chapter02` folder of this book's code bundle), as shown in the following code snippet:

```
In: t = dtype('Float64')
In: t.char
Out: 'd'
```

The `type` attribute corresponds to the type of object of array elements:

```
In: t.type
Out: <type 'numpy.float64'>
```

The `str` attribute of `dtype` gives a string representation of a data type. It starts with a character representing endianness, if appropriate, then a character code, followed by a number corresponding to the number of bytes that each array item requires. Here endianness means the way bytes are ordered within a 32- or 64-bit word. In the big-endian order, the most significant byte is stored first, which is indicated by '>'. In the little-endian order, the least significant byte is stored first, which is indicated by < as shown in the following lines of code:

```
In: t.str
Out: '<f8'
```

Creating a record data type

A record data type is a heterogeneous data type—think of it as representing a row in a spreadsheet or a database. To give an example of a record data type, we will create a record for a shop inventory. This record contains the name of an item represented by a 40-character string, the number of items in the store represented by a 32-bit integer, and finally, the price of the item represented by a 32-bit float. The following steps show how to create a record data type (see the `record.py` file in the `Chapter02` folder of this book's code bundle):

1. To create a record, check the following code snippet:
   ```
   In: t = dtype([('name', str_, 40), ('numitems', int32), ('price', float32)])
   In: t
   Out: dtype([('name', '|S40'), ('numitems', '<i4'),
     ('price', '<f4')])
   ```

2. To view the type of the field, check the following code snippet:

```
In: t['name']
Out: dtype('|S40')
```

If you don't give the `array()` function a data type, it will assume that it is dealing with floating point numbers. To create an array now, we really have to specify the data type as shown in the following lines of code; otherwise, we will get a `TypeError`:

```
In: itemz = array([('Meaning of life DVD', 42, 3.14), ('Butter', 13, 2.72)], dtype=t)
In: itemz[1]
Out: ('Butter', 13, 2.7200000286102295)
```

We created a record data type, which is a heterogeneous data type. The record contained a name as a character string, a number as an integer, and a price represented by a float value.

One-dimensional slicing and indexing

Slicing of one-dimensional NumPy arrays works just like slicing of Python lists. We can select a piece of an array from the index 3 to 7 that extracts the elements 3 through 6 (see the `slicing1d.py` file in the `Chapter02` folder of this book's code bundle), as shown in the following code snippet:

```
In: a = arange(9)
In: a[3:7]
Out: array([3, 4, 5, 6])
```

We can select elements from the index 0 to 7 with a step of two, as shown in the following lines of code:

```
In: a[:7:2]
Out: array([0, 2, 4, 6])
```

Just as in Python, we can use negative indices and reverse the array, as shown in the following lines of code:

```
In: a[::-1]
Out: array([8, 7, 6, 5, 4, 3, 2, 1, 0])
```

Manipulating array shapes

Another recurring task is flattening of arrays. Flattening in this context means transforming a multidimensional array into a one-dimensional array. In this example, we will demonstrate a number of ways to manipulate array shapes starting with flattening:

- `ravel()`: We can accomplish flattening with the `ravel()` function (see the `shapemanipulation.py` file in the `Chapter02` folder of this book's code bundle), as shown in the following code:

  ```
  In: b
  Out:
  array([[[ 0,  1,  2,  3],
          [ 4,  5,  6,  7],
          [ 8,  9, 10, 11]],
         [[12, 13, 14, 15],
          [16, 17, 18, 19],
          [20, 21, 22, 23]]])
  In: b.ravel()
  Out:
  array([ 0,  1,  2,  3,  4,  5,  6,  7,  8,  9, 10, 11, 12,
         13, 14, 15, 16, 17, 18, 19, 20, 21, 22, 23])
  ```

- `flatten()`: The appropriately-named function, `flatten()`, does the same as `ravel()`, but `flatten()` always allocates new memory, whereas `ravel()` might return a view of an array. This means that we can directly manipulate the array as follows:

  ```
  In: b.flatten()
  Out:
  array([ 0,  1,  2,  3,  4,  5,  6,  7,  8,  9, 10, 11, 12, 13, 14,
         15, 16,    17, 18, 19, 20, 21, 22, 23])
  ```

- `shape`: Besides the `reshape()` function, we can also set the shape directly with a tuple, which is shown as follows:

  ```
  In: b.shape = (6,4)
  In: b
  Out:
  array([[ 0,  1,  2,  3],
         [ 4,  5,  6,  7],
         [ 8,  9, 10, 11],
         [12, 13, 14, 15],
         [16, 17, 18, 19],
         [20, 21, 22, 23]])
  ```

  As you can see, this changes the array directly. Now we have a 6 x 4 array.

Chapter 2

- `transpose()`: In linear algebra, it is common to transpose matrices. We can do that too using the `transpose()` function, as shown in the following code:
  ```
  In: b.transpose()
  Out:
  array([[ 0,  4,  8, 12, 16, 20],
         [ 1,  5,  9, 13, 17, 21],
         [ 2,  6, 10, 14, 18, 22],
         [ 3,  7, 11, 15, 19, 23]])
  ```

- `resize()`: The `resize()` method works just like the `reshape()` method but modifies the array it operates on:
  ```
  In: b.resize((2,12))
  In: b
  Out:
  array([[ 0,  1,  2,  3,  4,  5,  6,  7,  8,  9, 10, 11],
         [12, 13, 14, 15, 16, 17, 18, 19, 20, 21, 22, 23]])
  ```

Stacking arrays

Arrays can be stacked horizontally, depth-wise, or vertically. We can use, for that purpose, the `vstack()`, `dstack()`, `hstack()`, `column_stack()`, `row_stack()`, and `concatenate()` functions. First, let's set up some arrays (see the `stacking.py` file in the `Chapter02` folder of this book's code bundle), as shown in the following code:

```
In: a = arange(9).reshape(3,3)
In: a
Out:
array([[0, 1, 2],
       [3, 4, 5],
       [6, 7, 8]])
In: b = 2 * a
In: b
Out:
array([[ 0,  2,  4],
       [ 6,  8, 10],
       [12, 14, 16]])
```

The following are the different types of stacking:

- **Horizontal stacking**: Starting with horizontal stacking, we will form a tuple of `ndarray` and give it to the `hstack()` function. This is shown as follows:
  ```
  In: hstack((a, b))
  Out:
  array([[ 0,  1,  2,  0,  2,  4],
         [ 3,  4,  5,  6,  8, 10],
         [ 6,  7,  8, 12, 14, 16]])
  ```

[29]

NumPy Basics

We can achieve the same with the `concatenate()` function, which is shown as follows:

```
In: concatenate((a, b), axis=1)
Out:
array([[ 0,  1,  2,  0,  2,  4],
       [ 3,  4,  5,  6,  8, 10],
       [ 6,  7,  8, 12, 14, 16]])
```

The following figure visualizes horizontal stacking:

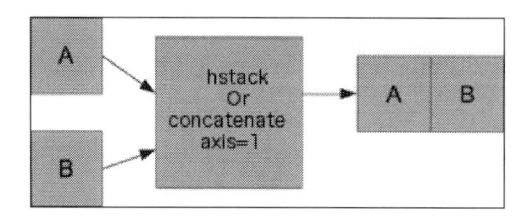

- **Vertical stacking**: With vertical stacking, again, a tuple is formed. This time, it is given to the `vstack()` function. This can be seen as follows:

```
In: vstack((a, b))
Out:
array([[ 0,  1,  2],
       [ 3,  4,  5],
       [ 6,  7,  8],
       [ 0,  2,  4],
       [ 6,  8, 10],
       [12, 14, 16]])
```

The `concatenate()` function produces the same result with the axis argument set to 0. This is the default value for the `axis` argument, as shown in the following code:

```
In: concatenate((a, b), axis=0)
Out:
array([[ 0,  1,  2],
       [ 3,  4,  5],
       [ 6,  7,  8],
       [ 0,  2,  4],
       [ 6,  8, 10],
       [12, 14, 16]])
```

Refer to the following diagram for vertical stacking:

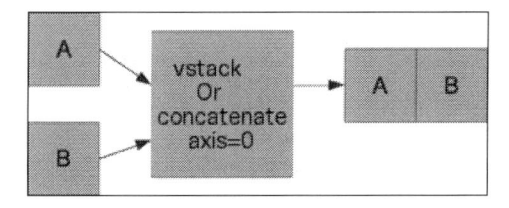

- **Depth stacking**: Additionally, there is depth-wise stacking using dstack() and a tuple, of course. This means stacking of a list of arrays along the third axis (depth). For instance, we could stack two-dimensional arrays of image data on top of each other:

```
In: dstack((a, b))
Out:
array([[[ 0,  0],
        [ 1,  2],
        [ 2,  4]],
       [[ 3,  6],
        [ 4,  8],
        [ 5, 10]],
       [[ 6, 12],
        [ 7, 14],
        [ 8, 16]]])
```

- **Column stacking**: The column_stack() function stacks one-dimensional arrays column-wise. It's shown as follows:

```
In: oned = arange(2)
In: oned
Out: array([0, 1])
In: twice_oned = 2 * oned
In: twice_oned
Out: array([0, 2])
In: column_stack((oned, twice_oned))
Out:
array([[0, 0],
       [1, 2]])
```

Two-dimensional arrays are stacked the way hstack() stacks them, as shown in the following code:

```
In: column_stack((a, b))
Out:
array([[ 0,  1,  2,  0,  2,  4],
       [ 3,  4,  5,  6,  8, 10],
       [ 6,  7,  8, 12, 14, 16]])
```

[31]

NumPy Basics

```
In: column_stack((a, b)) == hstack((a, b))
Out:
array([[ True, True, True, True, True, True],
       [ True, True, True, True, True, True],
       [ True, True, True, True, True, True]],
      dtype=bool)
```

Yes, you guessed it right! We compared two arrays with the == operator. Isn't this beautiful?

- **Row stacking**: NumPy, of course, also has a function that does row-wise stacking. It is called `row_stack()`, and for one-dimensional arrays, it just stacks the arrays in rows into a two-dimensional array:

```
In: row_stack((oned, twice_oned))
Out:
array([[0, 1],
       [0, 2]])
```

The `row_stack()` function results for two-dimensional arrays are equal to the `vstack()` function results, as follows:

```
In: row_stack((a, b))
Out:
array([[ 0,  1,  2],
       [ 3,  4,  5],
       [ 6,  7,  8],
       [ 0,  2,  4],
       [ 6,  8, 10],
       [12, 14, 16]])
In: row_stack((a,b)) == vstack((a, b))
Out:
array([[ True, True, True],
       [ True, True, True],
       [ True, True, True],
       [ True, True, True],
       [ True, True, True],
       [ True, True, True]], dtype=bool)
```

Splitting arrays

Arrays can be split vertically, horizontally, or depth-wise. The functions involved are `hsplit()`, `vsplit()`, `dsplit()`, and `split()`. We can either split arrays into arrays of the same shape or indicate the position after which the split should occur.

- **Horizontal splitting**: The ensuing code splits an array along its horizontal axis into three pieces of the same size and shape (see the `splitting.py` file in the `Chapter02` folder of this book's code bundle):

    ```
    In: a
    Out:
    array([[0, 1, 2],
           [3, 4, 5],
           [6, 7, 8]])
    In: hsplit(a, 3)
    Out:
    [array([[0],
           [3],
           [6]]),
     array([[1],
           [4],
           [7]]),
     array([[2],
           [5],
           [8]])]
    ```

    Compare it with a call of the `split()` function, with the extra parameter `axis=1`:

    ```
    In: split(a, 3, axis=1)
    Out:
    [array([[0],
           [3],
           [6]]),
     array([[1],
           [4],
           [7]]),
     array([[2],
           [5],
           [8]])]
    ```

NumPy Basics

- **Vertical splitting**: The `vsplit()` function splits an array along the vertical axis:

  ```
  In: vsplit(a, 3)
  Out: [array([[0, 1, 2]]), array([[3, 4, 5]]), array([[6, 7,
     8]])]
  ```

  The `split()` function, with `axis=0`, also splits an array along the vertical axis:

  ```
  In: split(a, 3, axis=0)
  Out: [array([[0, 1, 2]]), array([[3, 4, 5]]), array([[6, 7,
     8]])]
  ```

- **Depth-wise splitting**: The `dsplit()` function, unsurprisingly, splits an array depth-wise. We will need an array of rank three first:

  ```
  In: c = arange(27).reshape(3, 3, 3)
  In: c
  Out:
  array([[[ 0,  1,  2],
          [ 3,  4,  5],
          [ 6,  7,  8]],
         [[ 9, 10, 11],
          [12, 13, 14],
          [15, 16, 17]],
         [[18, 19, 20],
          [21, 22, 23],
          [24, 25, 26]]])
  In: dsplit(c, 3)
  Out:
  [array([[[ 0],
          [ 3],
          [ 6]],
         [[ 9],
          [12],
          [15]],
         [[18],
          [21],
          [24]]]),
   array([[[ 1],
          [ 4],
          [ 7]],
         [[10],
          [13],
          [16]],
         [[19],
          [22],
          [25]]]),
  ```

[34]

```
array([[[ 2],
        [ 5],
        [ 8]],
       [[11],
        [14],
        [17]],
       [[20],
        [23],
        [26]]])]
```

Array attributes

Besides the `shape` and `dtype` attributes, `ndarray` has a number of other attributes, as shown in the following list:

- `ndim`: This attribute gives the number of array dimensions (see the `arrayattributes2.py` file in the `Chapter02` folder of this book's code bundle):

  ```
  In: b
  Out:
  array([[ 0,  1,  2,  3,  4,  5,  6,  7,  8,  9, 10, 11],
         [12, 13, 14, 15, 16, 17, 18, 19, 20, 21, 22, 23]])
  In: b.ndim
  Out: 2
  ```

- `size`: This attribute displays the number of elements. This is shown as follows:

  ```
  In: b.size
  Out: 24
  ```

- `itemsize`: This attribute gives the number of bytes for each element in an array:

  ```
  In: b.itemsize
  Out: 8
  ```

- `nbytes`: This attribute gives the total number of bytes an array requires. It is just a product of the `itemsize` and `size` attributes:

  ```
  In: b.nbytes
  Out: 192
  In: b.size * b.itemsize
  Out: 192
  ```

NumPy Basics

- `T`: This attribute has the same effect as the `transpose()` function, which is shown as follows:

  ```
  In: b.resize(6,4)
  In: b
  Out:
  array([[ 0,  1,  2,  3],
         [ 4,  5,  6,  7],
         [ 8,  9, 10, 11],
         [12, 13, 14, 15],
         [16, 17, 18, 19],
         [20, 21, 22, 23]])
  In: b.T
  Out:
  array([[ 0,  4,  8, 12, 16, 20],
         [ 1,  5,  9, 13, 17, 21],
         [ 2,  6, 10, 14, 18, 22],
         [ 3,  7, 11, 15, 19, 23]])
  ```

  If the array has a rank lower than two, we will just get a view of the array:

  ```
  In: b.ndim
  Out: 1
  In: b.T
  Out: array([0, 1, 2, 3, 4])
  ```

  Complex numbers in NumPy are represented by 'j'. For example, we can create an array with complex numbers:

  ```
  In: b = array([1.j + 1, 2.j + 3])
  In: b
  Out: array([ 1.+1.j,  3.+2.j])
  ```

- `real`: This attribute gives us the real part of an array, or the array itself if it only contains real numbers:

  ```
  In: b.real
  Out: array([ 1.,  3.])
  ```

- `imag`: This attribute contains the imaginary part of an array:

  ```
  In: b.imag
  Out: array([ 1.,  2.])
  ```

  If the array contains complex numbers, then the data type is automatically also complex:

  ```
  In: b.dtype
  Out: dtype('complex128')
  In: b.dtype.str
  Out: '<c16'
  ```

[36]

Chapter 2

- `flat`: This attribute returns a `numpy.flatiter` object. This is the only way to acquire a `flatiter` — we do not have access to a `flatiter` constructor. The flat iterator enables us to loop through an array as if it is a flat array, as shown in the following code:

```
In: b = arange(4).reshape(2,2)
In: b
Out:
array([[0, 1],
       [2, 3]])
In: f = b.flat
In: f
Out: <numpy.flatiter object at 0x103013e00>
In: for item in f: print item
   .....:
0
1
2
3
```

It is possible to directly get an element with the `flatiter` object as follows:

```
In: b.flat[2]
Out: 2
```

It is also possible to get multiple elements as follows:

```
In: b.flat[[1,3]]
Out: array([1, 3])
```

The `flat` attribute is settable. Setting the value of the `flat` attribute leads to overwriting the values of the whole array as follows:

```
In: b.flat = 7
In: b
Out:
array([[7, 7],
       [7, 7]])
```

You can even get selected elements as follows:

```
In: b.flat[[1,3]] = 1
In: b
Out:
array([[7, 1],
       [7, 1]])
```

[37]

The following figure shows different attributes of ndarray:

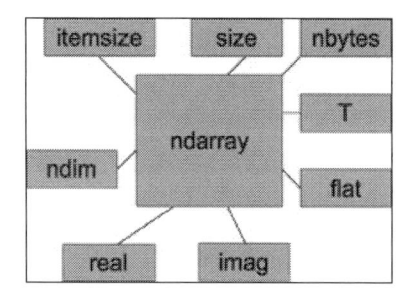

Converting arrays

We can convert a NumPy array to a Python list with the `tolist()` function (see the `arrayconversion.py` file in the `Chapter02` folder of this book's code bundle) as follows:

- To convert an array to a list, check the following code snippet:

    ```
    In: b
    Out: array([ 1.+1.j,  3.+2.j])
    In: b.tolist()
    Out: [(1+1j), (3+2j)]
    ```

- The `astype()` function converts an array to an array of the specified type as shown in the following code:

    ```
    In: b
    Out: array([ 1.+1.j,  3.+2.j])
    In: b.astype(int)
    /usr/local/bin/ipython:1: ComplexWarning: Casting complex values to real discards the imaginary part
      #!/usr/bin/python
    Out: array([1, 3])
    ```

> We are losing the imaginary part when casting from complex type to `int`.

The `astype()` function also accepts the name of a type as a string, as in the following snippet:

```
In: b.astype('complex')
Out: array([ 1.+1.j,  3.+2.j])
```

This won't show any warning this time, because we used the proper data type.

[38]

Creating views and copies

In the example about the `ravel()` function, views were mentioned. Views should not be confused with the concept of database views. Views in the NumPy world are not read-only, and you don't have the possibility to protect the underlying data. It is important to know when we are dealing with a shared array view and when we have a copy of array data. A slice, for instance, will create a view. This means that if you assign a slice to a variable and then change the underlying array, the value of this variable will change. We will create an array from the famous Lena image, copy the array, create a view, and at the end, modify the view. The Lena image array comes from a SciPy function.

1. To create a copy of the Lena array, the following line of code is used:

   `acopy = lena.copy()`

2. Now, to create a view of the array, use the following line of code:

   `aview = lena.view()`

3. Set all the values of the view to 0 with a flat iterator, as follows:

   `aview.flat = 0`

The end result is that only one of the images shows the Playboy model. The other ones got censored completely, as shown in the following figure.

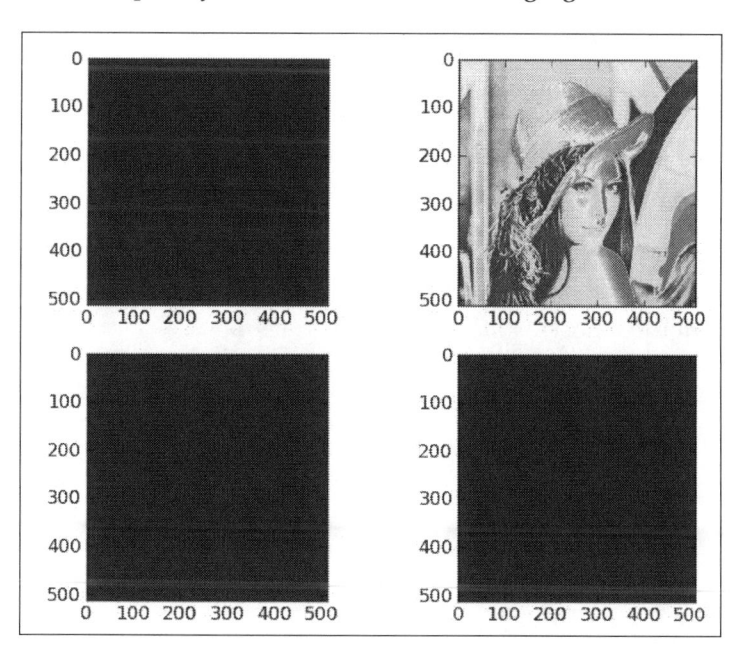

NumPy Basics

Refer to the following code of this section (without comments to save space; for the complete code, see the `copy_view.py` file in the `Chapter02` folder of this book's code bundle) showing the behavior of array views and copies:

```
import scipy.misc
import matplotlib.pyplot as plt

lena = scipy.misc.lena()
acopy = lena.copy()
aview = lena.view()
plt.subplot(221)
plt.imshow(lena)
plt.subplot(222)
plt.imshow(acopy)
plt.subplot(223)
plt.imshow(aview)
aview.flat = 0
plt.subplot(224)
plt.imshow(aview)
plt.show()
```

As you can see, by changing the view at the end of the program, we changed the original Lena array. This resulted in having three blue (or black if you are looking at a black and white image) images. The copied array was unaffected. It is important to remember that views are not read-only.

Fancy indexing

Fancy indexing is indexing that does not involve integers or slices, which is normal indexing. In this section, we will apply fancy indexing to set the diagonal values of the Lena image to 0. This will draw black lines along the diagonals, crossing it through, not because there is something wrong with the image, but just as an exercise. Perform the following steps for fancy indexing:

1. Set the values of the first diagonal to 0. To set the diagonal values to 0, we need to define two different ranges for the x and y values as follows:

   ```
   lena[range(xmax), range(ymax)] = 0
   ```

2. Now, set the values of the other diagonal to 0. To set the values of the other diagonal, we require a different set of ranges, but the principles stay the same, as follows:

   ```
   lena[range(xmax-1,-1,-1), range(ymax)] = 0
   ```

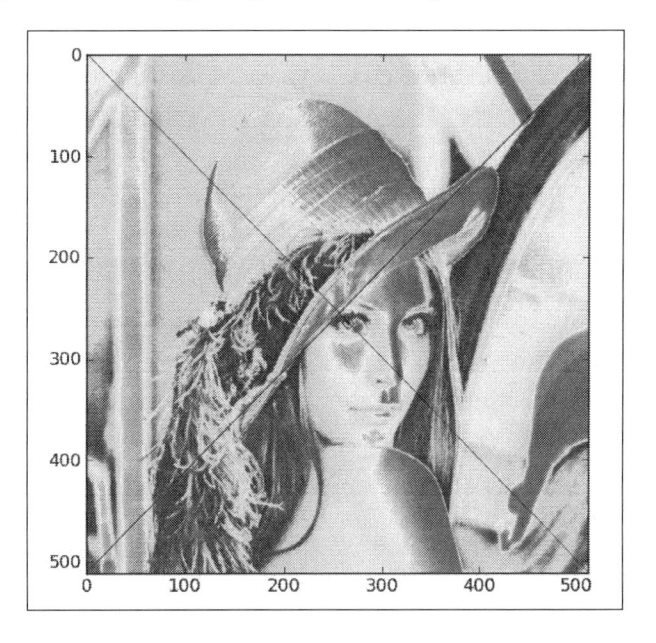

At the end we get the following image with the diagonals crossed out:

The following code for this section is without comments. The complete code for this is in the `fancy.py` file in the `Chapter02` folder of this book's code bundle.

```
import scipy.misc
import matplotlib.pyplot as plt

lena = scipy.misc.lena()
xmax = lena.shape[0]
ymax = lena.shape[1]
lena[range(xmax), range(ymax)] = 0
lena[range(xmax-1,-1,-1), range(ymax)] = 0
plt.imshow(lena)
plt.show()
```

We defined separate ranges for the x and y values. These ranges were used to index the Lena array. Fancy indexing is performed based on an internal NumPy iterator object. This can be achieved by performing the following three steps:

1. The iterator object is created.
2. The iterator object gets bound to the array.
3. Array elements are accessed via the iterator.

Indexing with a list of locations

Let's use the `ix_()` function to shuffle the Lena image. This function creates a mesh from multiple sequences. As arguments, we give one-dimensional sequences, and the function returns a tuple of NumPy arrays. For example, check the following code snippet:

```
In : ix_([0,1], [2,3])
Out:
(array([[0],
        [1]]), array([[2, 3]]))
```

To index the array with a list of locations, perform the following steps:

1. Shuffle the array indices. Create a random indices array with the `shuffle()` function of the `numpy.random` module, as shown in the following lines of code. The function changes the array `inplace` by the way.

   ```
   def shuffle_indices(size):
       arr = np.arange(size)
       np.random.shuffle(arr)

       return arr
   ```

2. Now plot the shuffled indices as follows:

   ```
   plt.imshow(lena[np.ix_(xindices, yindices)])
   ```

What we get is a completely scrambled Lena, as shown in the following image:

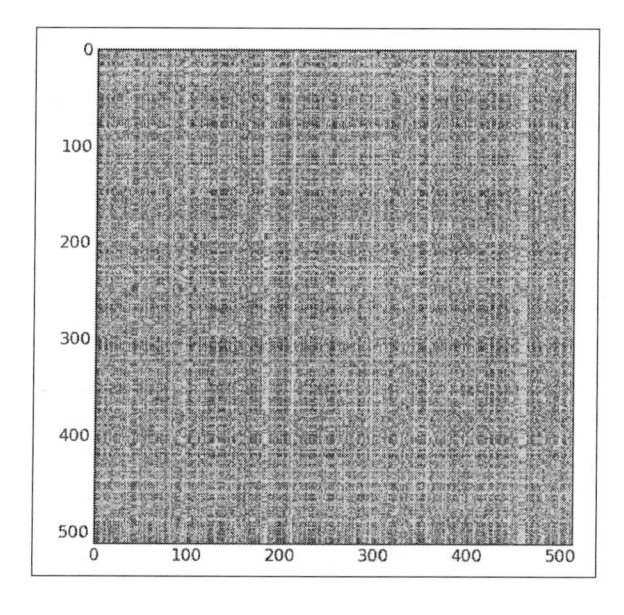

Chapter 2

The following code for this section is without comments. The complete code for this can be found in the ix.py file in the Chapter02 folder of this book's code bundle.

```
import scipy.misc
import matplotlib.pyplot
import numpy as np

lena = scipy.misc.lena()
xmax = lena.shape[0]
ymax = lena.shape[1]

def shuffle_indices(size):
    arr = np.arange(size)
    np.random.shuffle(arr)

    return arr

xindices = shuffle_indices(xmax)
np.testing.assert_equal(len(xindices), xmax)
yindices = shuffle_indices(ymax)
np.testing.assert_equal(len(yindices), ymax)
plt.imshow(lena[np.ix_(xindices, yindices)])
plt.show()
```

Indexing arrays with Booleans

Boolean indexing is indexing based on a Boolean array and falls in the category of fancy indexing. Since Boolean indexing is a form of fancy indexing, the way it works is basically the same. This means that indexing happens with the help of a special iterator object. Perform the following steps to index an array:

1. First, we create an image with dots on the diagonal. This is in some way similar to the *Fancy indexing* section. This time we select modulo four points on the diagonal of the image, as shown in the following code snippet:

   ```
   def get_indices(size):
       arr = np.arange(size)
       return arr % 4 == 0
   ```

2. Then we just apply this selection and plot the points, as shown in the following code snippet:

   ```
   lena1 = lena.copy()
   xindices = get_indices(lena.shape[0])
   yindices = get_indices(lena.shape[1])
   lena1[xindices, yindices] = 0
   plt.subplot(211)
   plt.imshow(lena1)
   ```

[43]

NumPy Basics

3. Select array values between a quarter and three-quarters of the maximum value, and set them to `0`, as shown in the following line of code:

   ```
   lena2[(lena > lena.max()/4) & (lena < 3 * lena.max()/4)] = 0
   ```

The plot with the two new images is shown as follows:

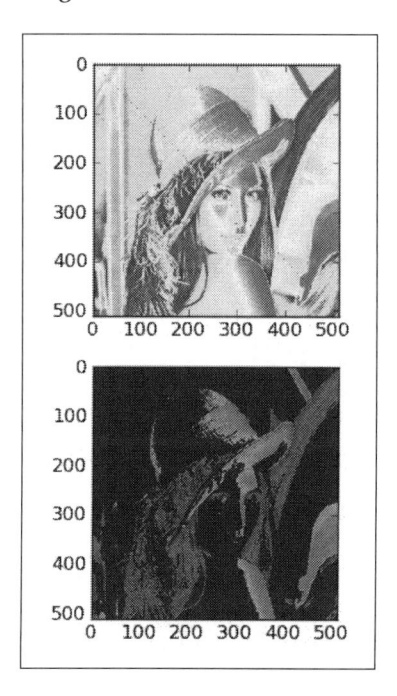

The following is the code for this section (see the `boolean_indexing.py` file in the `Chapter02` folder of this book's code bundle):

```
import scipy.misc
import matplotlib.pyplot as plt
import numpy as np

lena = scipy.misc.lena()

def get_indices(size):
    arr = np.arange(size)
    return arr % 4 == 0

lena1 = lena.copy()
```

```
xindices = get_indices(lena.shape[0])
yindices = get_indices(lena.shape[1])
lena1[xindices, yindices] = 0
plt.subplot(211)
plt.imshow(lena1)
lena2 = lena.copy()
lena2[(lena > lena.max()/4) & (lena < 3 * lena.max()/4)] = 0
plt.subplot(212)
plt.imshow(lena2)
plt.show()
```

Stride tricks for Sudoku

We can do even more fancy things with NumPy. The `ndarray` class has a field, `strides`, which is a tuple indicating the number of bytes to step in each dimension when going through an array. Sudoku is a popular puzzle originally from Japan; although it was known in a similar form before in other countries. If you don't know about Sudoku, it's maybe better that way because it is highly addictive. Let's apply some stride tricks to the problem of splitting a Sudoku puzzle to the 3 x 3 squares it is composed of:

1. First define the Sudoku puzzle array, as shown in the following code snippet. This one is filled with the contents of the actual solved Sudoku puzzle (part of the array is omitted for brevity).

   ```
   sudoku = np.array([
       [2, 8, 7, 1, 6, 5, 9, 4, 3],
       [9, 5, 4, 7, 3, 2, 1, 6, 8],
       ...
       [7, 3, 6, 2, 8, 4, 5, 1, 9]
   ])
   ```

2. Now calculate the strides. The `itemsize` field of `ndarray` gives us the number of bytes in an array. `itemsize` calculates the strides as follows:

   ```
   strides = sudoku.itemsize * np.array([27, 3, 9, 1])
   ```

3. Now we can split the puzzle into squares with the `as_strided()` function of the `np.lib.stride_tricks` module, as shown in the following lines of code:

   ```
   squares = np.lib.stride_tricks.as_strided(sudoku, shape=shape, strides=strides)
   print(squares)
   ```

NumPy Basics

This prints separate Sudoku squares (some of the squares were omitted to save space), as follows:

```
[[[[2 8 7]
   [9 5 4]
   [6 1 3]]
  ...
  [[8 7 9]
   [4 2 1]
   [3 6 5]]
  ...

  [[1 9 8]
   [5 4 2]
   [7 3 6]]
  ...
  [[4 2 6]
   [3 8 7]
   [5 1 9]]]]
```

The following is the complete source code for this example (see the strides.py file in the Chapter02 folder of this book's code bundle):

```
import numpy as np

sudoku = np.array([
    [2, 8, 7, 1, 6, 5, 9, 4, 3],
    [9, 5, 4, 7, 3, 2, 1, 6, 8],
    [6, 1, 3, 8, 4, 9, 7, 5, 2],
    [8, 7, 9, 6, 5, 1, 2, 3, 4],
    [4, 2, 1, 3, 9, 8, 6, 7, 5],
    [3, 6, 5, 4, 2, 7, 8, 9, 1],
    [1, 9, 8, 5, 7, 3, 4, 2, 6],
    [5, 4, 2, 9, 1, 6, 3, 8, 7],
    [7, 3, 6, 2, 8, 4, 5, 1, 9]
    ])

shape = (3, 3, 3, 3)
strides = sudoku.itemsize * np.array([27, 3, 9, 1])
squares = np.lib.stride_tricks.as_strided(sudoku, shape=shape, strides=strides)
print(squares)
```

We applied stride tricks to decompose a Sudoku puzzle in its constituent 3 x 3 squares. The strides tell us how many bytes we need to skip at each step when going through the Sudoku array.

Broadcasting arrays

In a nutshell, NumPy tries to perform an operation even though the operands do not have the same shape. In this section, we will multiply an array and a scalar. The scalar is extended to the shape of an array operand, and then the multiplication is performed. We will download an audio file and make a new version that is quieter:

1. First, read the WAV file. We will use standard Python code to download an audio file of Austin Powers saying "Smashing, baby". SciPy has a `wavfile` module that allows you to load sound data or generate WAV files. If SciPy is installed, then we should already have this module. The `read()` function returns a data array and sample rate. In this example, we only care about the data.

   ```
   sample_rate, data = scipy.io.wavfile.read(WAV_FILE)
   ```

2. Plot the original WAV data with Matplotlib. Give the subplot the title, `Original`, as shown in the following lines of code:

   ```
   plt.subplot(2, 1, 1)
   plt.title("Original")
   plt.plot(data)
   ```

3. Now create a new array. We will use NumPy to make a quieter audio sample. It is just a matter of creating a new array with smaller values by multiplying with a constant. This is where the magic of broadcasting occurs. At the end, we need to make sure that we have the same data type as in the original array because of the WAV format.

   ```
   newdata = data * 0.2
   newdata = newdata.astype(np.uint8)
   ```

4. Now this new array can be written into a new WAV file as follows:

   ```
   scipy.io.wavfile.write("quiet.wav",
       sample_rate, newdata)
   ```

5. Plot the new data array with Matplotlib as follows:

   ```
   matplotlib.pyplot.subplot(2, 1, 2)
   matplotlib.pyplot.title("Quiet")
   matplotlib.pyplot.plot(newdata)
   matplotlib.pyplot.show()
   ```

NumPy Basics

The result is a plot of the original WAV file data and a new array with smaller values, as shown in the following figure:

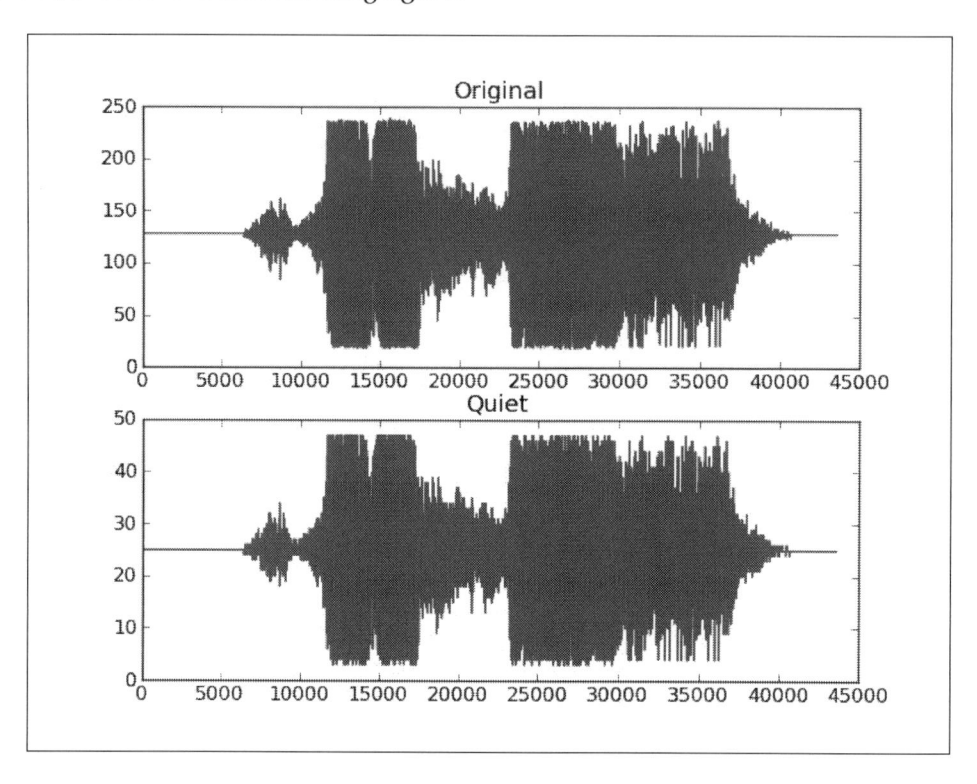

The following is the complete code for this section (see the broadcasting.py file in the `Chapter02` folder of this book's code bundle):

```
import scipy.io.wavfile
import matplotlib.pyplot
import urllib2
import numpy as np

response = urllib2.urlopen('http://www.thesoundarchive.com/
austinpowers/smashingbaby.wav')
print response.info()
WAV_FILE = 'smashingbaby.wav'
filehandle = open(WAV_FILE, 'w')
filehandle.write(response.read())
filehandle.close()
sample_rate, data = scipy.io.wavfile.read(WAV_FILE)
print "Data type", data.dtype, "Shape", data.shape
plt.subplot(2, 1, 1)
```

```
plt.title("Original")
plt.plot(data)
newdata = data * 0.2
newdata = newdata.astype(np.uint8)
print "Data type", newdata.dtype, "Shape", newdata.shape
scipy.io.wavfile.write("quiet.wav",
    sample_rate, newdata)
plt.subplot(2, 1, 2)
plt.title("Quiet")
plt.plot(newdata)
plt.show()
```

Summary

We learned a lot in this chapter about the NumPy fundamentals: data types and arrays. Arrays have several attributes describing them. We learned that one of these attributes is the data type which, in NumPy, is represented by a full-fledged object.

NumPy arrays can be sliced and indexed in an efficient manner, just as in the case of Python lists. NumPy arrays have the added ability of working with multiple dimensions.

The shape of an array can be manipulated in many ways, such as stacking, resizing, reshaping, and splitting. A great number of convenience functions for shape manipulation were demonstrated in this chapter.

Having learned about the basics, it's time to move on to data analysis with commonly used functions in *Chapter 3, Basic Data Analysis with NumPy*. This includes the usage of basic statistical and mathematical functions.

3
Basic Data Analysis with NumPy

In this chapter, we will learn about basic data analysis through an example of historical weather data. We will learn about functions that make working with NumPy easier.

In this chapter, we shall cover the following topics:

- Functions working on arrays
- Loading arrays from files containing weather data
- Simple mathematical and statistical functions

Introducing the dataset

First, we will learn about file I/O with NumPy. Data is usually stored in files. You would not get far if you are not able to read from and write to files.

The **Royal Netherlands Meteorological Institute (KNMI)** offers daily weather data online (browse to `http://www.knmi.nl/climatology/daily_data/download.html`). KNMI is the Dutch meteorological service headquartered in De Bilt. Let's download one of the KNMI files from the De Bilt weather station. The file is roughly 10 megabytes. It has some text with explanation about the data in Dutch and English. Below that is the data in comma-separated values format. I separated the metadata and the actual data into separate files. The separation is not necessary because you can skip rows when loading from NumPy. I wrote a simple script with NumPy to determine the maximum and minimum temperature for the dataset from a CSV file that was created in the separation process.

Basic Data Analysis with NumPy

The temperatures are given in tenths of a degree Celsius. There are three columns containing temperatures:

- An average temperature for a 24-hour period
- The daily minimum temperature
- The daily maximum temperature

We will ignore the average temperatures for now. Also notice that there were missing values, so let's convert them to the **Not a Number** (**NaN**) value. NaN is a special value for floating point numbers in Python. In the end, we can come up with the following simple script (see the `intro.py` file in the `Chapter03` folder of this book's code bundle):

```
import numpy as np
import sys

to_float = lambda x: float(x.strip() or np.nan)

# Measurements are in tenths of degrees
min_temp, max_temp = np.loadtxt(sys.argv[1], delimiter=',',
   usecols=(12, 14), unpack=True, converters={12: to_float, 14:
   to_float}) * .1
print "# Records", len(min_temp), len(max_temp)
print "Minimum", np.nanmin(min_temp)
print "Maximum", np.nanmax(max_temp)
```

This script prints the number of records and the minimum and maximum temperature:

```
# Records 40996 40996
Minimum -24.8
Maximum 36.8
```

> We read a file with the `loadtxt` function. By default, `loadtxt` tries to convert all data into floats. The `loadtxt` function has a special parameter for this purpose. The parameter is called `converters` and is a dictionary that links columns with the so-called converter functions. We also specified comma as the delimiter for fields and columns to use. Please refer to http://docs.scipy.org/doc/numpy/reference/generated/numpy.loadtxt.html for more details. KNMI quotes the temperature values in tenths of a degree Celsius, so a simple multiplication was required. The `nanmin` and `nanmax` functions do the same as the NumPy `max` and `min` functions, but they also ignore NaNs.

Determining the daily temperature range

The daily temperature range, or diurnal temperature variation as it is called in meteorology, is not so big a deal on Earth. In desert areas on Earth or generally on different planets, the variation is greater. We will have a look at the daily temperature range for the data we downloaded in the previous example:

1. To analyze temperature ranges, we will need to import the NumPy package and the NumPy masked arrays:

   ```
   import numpy as np
   import sys
   import numpy.ma as ma
   from datetime import datetime as dt
   ```

2. We will load a bit more data than that loaded in the previous section: dates of measurements in the YYYYMMDD format and the average daily temperature. Dates require special conversion. Firstly date strings are converted to dates and then to numbers as follows:

   ```
   to_float = lambda x: float(x.strip() or np.nan)
   to_date = lambda x: dt.strptime(x, "%Y%m%d").toordinal()

   dates, avg_temp, min_temp, max_temp =
     np.loadtxt(sys.argv[1], delimiter=',', usecols=(1, 11,
     12, 14), unpack=True, converters={1: to_date, 12:
     to_float, 14: to_float})
   ```

3. Let's calculate the percentage of days that minimum and maximum temperatures are below zero degrees Celsius (freezing point):

   ```
   print "% days min < 0", 100 * len(min_temp[min_temp <
     0])/float(len(min_temp))
   print "% days max < 0", 100 * len(max_temp[max_temp <
     0])/float(len(max_temp))
   ```

   The chance of the maximum daily temperature being below zero seems to be three percent. That's about 10 days per year. The minimum daily temperature is more likely to be below zero, with a likelihood of 18 percent. This comes to approximately two months a year. Not consecutive months obviously.

   % days min below 0 18.1944579959
   % days max below 0 2.81978729632

   Unfortunately, we still have the problem of missing values. One way to deal with this is to use masked arrays. Masked arrays are a special type of NumPy array that usually contain missing, invalid, or suspect values.

4. Now, to solve the missing values problem, just give a masked array a mask created with the `isnan` function. We will calculate averages and standard deviations for temperatures and minimum and maximum for daily temperature ranges:

```
ranges = max_temp - min_temp
print "Minimum daily range", np.nanmin(ranges)
print "Maximum daily range", np.nanmax(ranges)

masked_ranges = ma.array(ranges, mask = np.isnan(ranges))
print "Average daily range", masked_ranges.mean()
print "Standard deviation", masked_ranges.std()

masked_mins = ma.array(min_temp, mask = np.isnan(min_temp))
print "Average minimum temperature", masked_mins.mean(),
  "Standard deviation", masked_mins.std()

masked_maxs = ma.array(max_temp, mask = np.isnan(max_temp))
print "Average maximum temperature", masked_maxs.mean(),
  "Standard deviation", masked_maxs.std()
```

Apparently, the average daily range is eight degrees, while the average minimum is around five degrees, and the average maximum is around 13 degrees. The following values were printed at the time the code was written; naturally, if you run the program with more recent data, the outcome can differ a bit:

```
Minimum daily range 0.6
Maximum daily range 22.2
Average daily range 8.20358580315
Standard deviation 3.72983839106
Average minimum temperature 5.39096231248
Standard deviation 5.85061308004
Average maximum temperature 13.5945481156
Standard deviation 7.40767291657
```

You can find the code for this example in the `daily_temperature_range.py` file in the `Chapter03` folder of this book's code bundle.

Chapter 3

Looking for evidence of global warming

According to the global warming theory, the temperature on Earth has increased on average since the end of the 19th century. During the last century until now, the temperature supposedly has gained about 0.8 degrees. Apparently, most of this warming has happened in the last two or three decades. In the future, we can expect the temperature to rise even more, leading to droughts, heat waves, and other unpleasant phenomena. Obviously, some regions will be hit harder than others. Several solutions have been proposed, including reduction of greenhouse gas emissions and geo-engineering by spreading special gases in the atmosphere in order to reflect more sunlight.

The data we downloaded from the Dutch Meteorological Institute, KNMI, is not sufficient to prove whether global warming is real or not, but we can certainly examine it further. For instance, we can check whether the temperature in De Bilt (that's where the data was collected) in the first half of the dataset is lower than in the second half. Another thing we can do is plot yearly average temperatures. De Bilt by the way, as far as I know, is a small town in central Netherlands without heavy industry. We need to import NumPy and Matplotlib to create plots later on. Perform the following steps to calculate the yearly average temperature:

1. We will load the average daily temperatures and the corresponding dates. Actually, we will convert the dates to years immediately to be able to calculate yearly average temperatures:

   ```
   to_year = lambda x: dt.strptime(x, "%Y%m%d").year

   years, avg_temp = np.loadtxt(sys.argv[1], delimiter=',',
     usecols=(1, 11), unpack=True, converters={1: to_year})

   # Measurements are in .1 degrees Celsius
   avg_temp = .1 * avg_temp

   N = len(avg_temp)
   print "First Year", years[0], "Last Year", years[-1]
   assert N == len(years)
   assert years[:N/2].mean() < years[N/2:].mean()
   ```

   As you can see, some sanity checking occurs at the end of the snippet, which prints the following output:

   First Year 1901.0 Last Year 2013.0

2. After dividing the average daily temperature values in two halves, we can calculate and compare the arithmetic means of both halves. Here, we are using the NumPy ndarray methods to compare the standard deviation as well:

   ```
   print "First half average", avg_temp[:N/2].mean(), "Std Dev",
     avg_temp[:N/2].std()
   print "Second half average", avg_temp[N/2:].mean(), "Std Dev",
     avg_temp[N/2:].std()
   ```

   This gives us the following output:

   ```
   First half average 9.19078446678 Std Dev 6.42457006016
   Second half average 9.78066152795 Std Dev 6.34152195332
   ```

   It seems that the average temperature is slightly higher in the second half of the dataset.

3. Computing yearly average temperatures is simple. For each year, find the array indices using the `where` function corresponding to that year. With the indices, we then calculate the mean for each year and store it:

   ```
   avgs = []
   year_range = range(int(years[0]), int(years[-1]) - 1)

   for year in year_range:
       indices = np.where(years == year)
       avgs.append(avg_temp[indices].mean())

   plt.plot(year_range, avgs, 'r-', label="Yearly Averages")
   plt.plot(year_range, np.ones(len(avgs)) * np.mean(avgs))
   plt.legend(prop={'size':'x-small'})
   plt.show()
   ```

   We get the following plot as a result. For comparison, an average of all average temperatures is also drawn through the middle of the plot. Notice how the yearly average temperatures seem to be on the rise from 1980 onwards (refer to the `global_warming.py` file in the `Chapter03` folder of this book's code bundle).

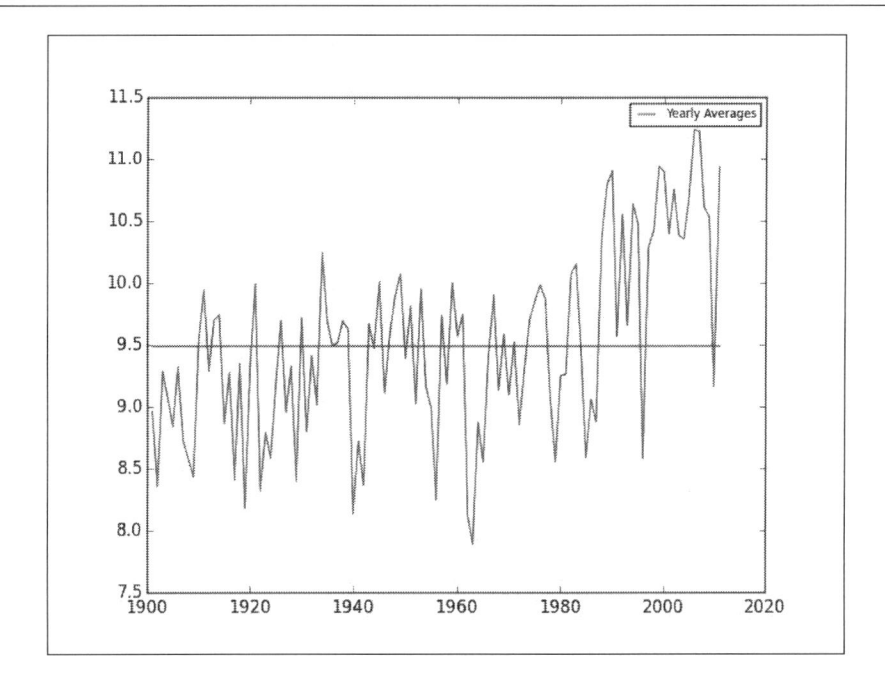

[Yearly Averages chart, 1900–2020, values ranging approximately 7.5 to 11.5]

Comparing solar radiation versus temperature

The Sun is of course a very important factor when it comes to temperature. Unfortunately, the De Bilt dataset from the KNMI is missing a lot of data concerning the Sun's radiation. The data is given in Joule per square centimeter. There are also other variables in the file, which are derived from solar radiation, such as the sunshine duration in hours.

We are going to analyze the radiation data a bit, draw a histogram, and compare it with the daily average temperatures. To compare, we will calculate the correlation coefficient between radiation and temperature and plot yearly relative changes in average temperature and radiation. Originally it seemed a good idea to have a scatter plot, but that didn't look right with thousands of data points, so instead, it was decided to compress the data as it were. Later, the author realized that radiation was present from around 1960 onwards, so it might have been better to plot the correlations coefficient for each year. This is left as an exercise for the reader.

Basic Data Analysis with NumPy

We need to import NumPy, the NumPy masked array module, and Matplotlib. The steps to compare solar radiation versus temperature are presented as follows:

1. We will load the dates and convert them to years, and then load the average temperature and radiation. The latter misses a lot of values, so we will convert the missing values to NaN and then create a masked array out of the radiation data:

    ```
    to_float = lambda x: float(x.strip() or np.nan)
    to_year = lambda x: dt.strptime(x, "%Y%m%d").year

    years, avg_temp, Q = np.loadtxt(sys.argv[1], delimiter=',',
    usecols=(1, 11, 20), unpack=True, converters={1: to_year, 20: to_
    float})
    ma
    # Measurements are in .1 degrees Celsius
    avg_temp = .1 * avg_temp

    Q = ma.masked_invalid(Q)
    ```

2. We will have a look at the minimum, maximum, mean, and standard deviation of radiation. Additionally, we will print the correlation coefficient of temperature and radiation with the `corrcoef` function. To compute the coefficient, we need to match the data properly by avoiding the NaN values. Also, we have to get one of the off-diagonal values of the correlation matrix that NumPy returns. The `compressed` method of masked arrays returns all the nonmasked data as a one-dimensional array:

    ```
    print "# temperature values", len(avg_temp), "# radiation values",
    len(Q.compressed())
    print "Radiation Min", Q.min(), "Radiation Max", Q.max()
    print "Radiation Average", Q.compressed().mean(), "Std
      Dev", Q.std()

    match_temp = avg_temp[np.logical_not(np.isnan(Q))]
    print "Correlation Coefficient", np.corrcoef(match_temp,
      Q.compressed())[0][1]
    ```

    The script prints the following output:

    ```
    # temperature values 40996 # radiation values 20361
    Radiation Min 7.0 Radiation Max 3081.0
    Radiation Average 957.156082707 Std Dev 740.68047373
    Correlation Coefficient 0.62767320286
    ```

    As you can see, the correlation is not that strong.

3. We already did yearly averaging. Now we add radiation to be averaged yearly. Another thing that we want to do is calculate the relative change of the variables we are interested in as percentages. The `diff` function gives us by default the first order difference between neighboring array values:

   ```
   avg_temps = []
   avg_qs = []
   year_range = range(int(years[0]), int(years[-1]) - 1)

   for year in year_range:
       indices = np.where(years == year)
       avg_temps.append(avg_temp[indices].mean())
       avg_qs.append(Q[indices].mean())

   def percents(a):
       return 100 * np.diff(a)/a[:-1]
   ```

4. We will plot the radiation histogram and relative changes in yearly average temperature and radiation with Matplotlib. Matplotlib is an open source Python plotting library considered by many as part of the basic stack. For more information, please refer to *Matplotlib for Python Developers, Packt Publishing*. The second edition of this book was coauthored by the author of this book and should be published in 2014.

   ```
   plt.subplot(211)
   plt.title("Global Radiation Histogram")
   plt.hist(Q.compressed(), 200)

   plt.subplot(212)
   plt.title("Changes in Average Yearly Temperature & Radiation")
   plt.plot(year_range[1:], percents(avg_temps), label='% Change Temperature')
   plt.plot(year_range[1:], percents(avg_qs), label='% Change Radiation')
   plt.legend(prop={'size':'x-small'})
   plt.show()
   ```

The Matplotlib `subplot` function creates a tableau or grid from multiple plots. In this example, we used 211 to indicate that there will be two plots, and that we want this particular plot to be placed in the first row in the first column. Similarly, 212 means put the plot on second row in the first column. Refer to the following plots and the `solar_radiation.py` file in the `Chapter03` folder of this book's code bundle:

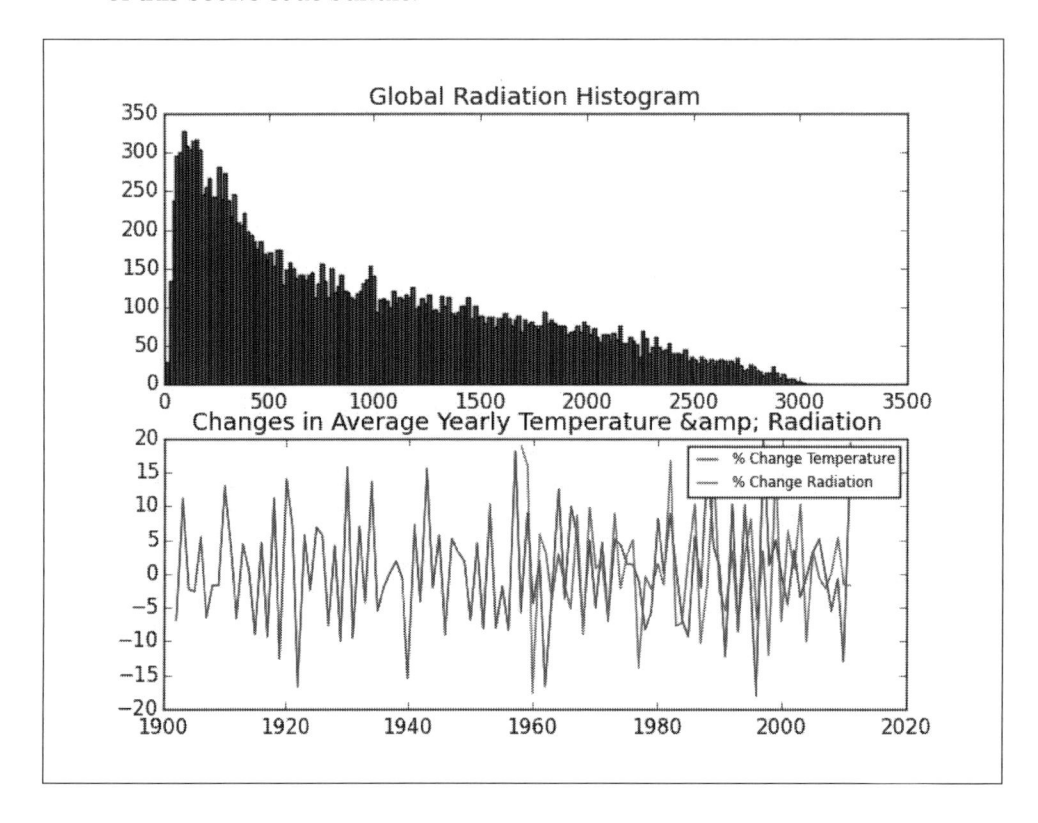

Analyzing wind direction

Wind is the movement of air due to the difference in atmospheric pressure. The KNMI De Bilt data file has a column for the vector mean wind direction in degrees (360 = north, 90 = east, 180 = south, 270 = west, 0 = calm/variable). We will plot a histogram of that data and compute the corresponding average temperature for each wind direction. It seems reasonable to expect that the direction from which the wind originates influences temperature. In other words, some locations tend to be warmer or colder, so air emanating from there will be warmer or colder, respectively. The Netherlands, as you may know, doesn't have any mountains, so we don't have to take that into account. We do have to remind ourselves of the proximity of the North Sea. The Netherlands has a moderate maritime climate with southwestern winds. We can study the wind direction information with the following procedure:

1. We will load the wind direction and average temperatures into NumPy arrays. Wind direction has missing values, so some conversion is in order. We will create a masked array from the wind direction values:

    ```
    to_float = lambda x: float(x.strip() or np.nan)
    wind_direction, avg_temp = np.loadtxt(sys.argv[1], delimiter=',',
       usecols=(2, 11), unpack=True, converters={2: to_float})
    wind_direction = ma.masked_invalid(wind_direction)
    ```

2. We can average wind directions the way we calculated the average of years by going over each of the possible wind directions, finding the corresponding temperature values, and averaging them:

    ```
    avgs = []

    for direction in xrange(360):
        indices = np.where(direction == wind_direction)
        avgs.append(avg_temp[indices].mean())
    ```

3. Now, we will plot the wind direction histogram and average temperatures per wind direction as follows:

    ```
    plt.subplot(211)
    plt.title("Wind Direction Histogram")
    plt.hist(wind_direction.compressed(), 200)

    plt.subplot(212)
    plt.title("Average Temperature vs Wind Direction")
    plt.plot(np.arange(360), avgs)
    plt.show()
    ```

We get the following plots as a result. Notice the peak in the histogram that corresponds to a southwestern wind direction. The average temperature seems to be bottoming around 50 degrees.

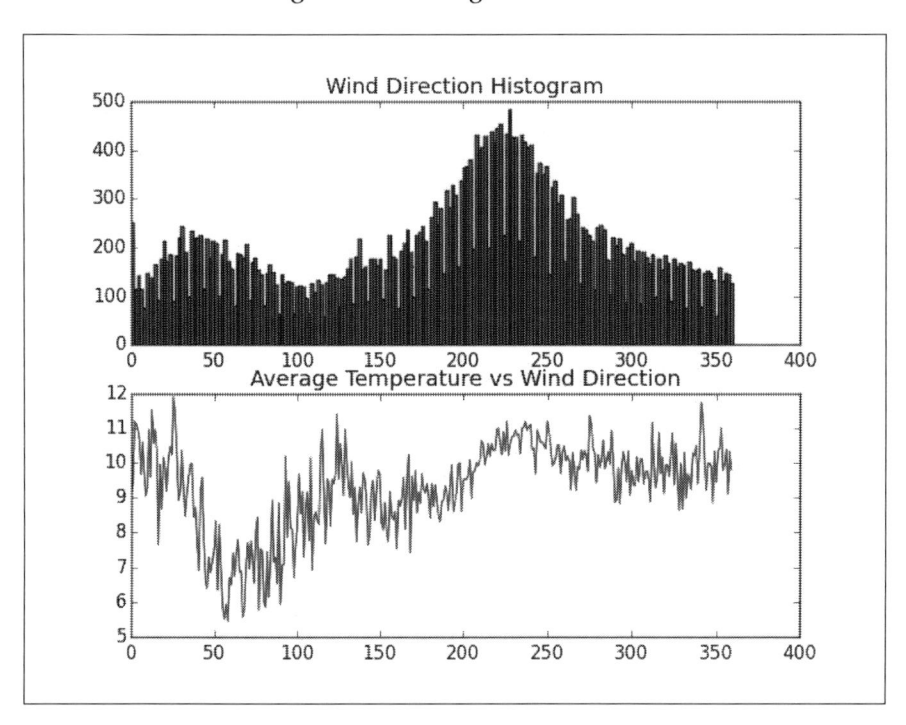

Analyzing wind speed

Wind speed is a very important value. The KNMI De Bilt data file has daily average wind speed data expressed in meters per second as well.

We will load the wind direction, wind speed, and average temperature into NumPy arrays. Wind direction and speed have missing values, so some conversion is in order. We will create a masked array from the wind direction and speed values:

```
to_float = lambda x: float(x.strip() or np.nan)
wind_direction, wind_speed, avg_temp =
  np.loadtxt(sys.argv[1], delimiter=',', usecols=(2, 4,
  11), unpack=True, converters={2: to_float, 4: to_float})
wind_direction = ma.masked_invalid(wind_direction)
wind_speed = ma.masked_invalid(wind_speed)
print "# Wind Speed values", len(wind_speed.compressed())
print "Min speed", wind_speed.min(), "Max speed",
  wind_speed.max()
```

```
print "Average", wind_speed.mean(), "Std. Dev",
    wind_speed.std()

print "Correlation of wind speed and temperature",
    np.corrcoef(avg_temp[~wind_speed.mask],
    wind_speed.compressed())[0][1]
```

> We will go through the usual statistics of wind speed—minimum, maximum, average, standard deviation, and correlation with average temperatures. Note that for the correlation computation, we need to match the average temperature values with the valid wind speed values. We do that by negating the mask of the wind speed array, giving us the indices of valid values.

In the output, we see a weak negative correlation between wind speed and temperature as follows:

```
# Wind Speed values 39871
Min speed 0.0
Max speed 16.5
Average 4.2211381706
Std. Dev 1.93906822268
Correlation of wind speed and temperature -0.126166541437
```

Analyzing precipitation and sunshine duration

The KNMI De Bilt data file has a column containing precipitation duration values in 0.1 hours. The sunshine duration also given in 0.1 hours is derived from global radiation values. Notice the use of the word *global* and not *solar*. Hence, there are other sources of radiation taken into account here, but details are not very important right now. We will plot a histogram of precipitation duration values. However, we will omit the days when no rain fell, because there are so many dry days that it skews the overall picture. We will also display the monthly average precipitation and sunshine durations. The following steps describe the rainfall and sunlight length study:

1. We will load the dates converted into months, sunshine, and precipitation duration into NumPy arrays. Again, we convert missing values to NaN. The code is as follows:

    ```
    to_float = lambda x: float(x.strip() or np.nan)
    to_month = lambda x: dt.strptime(x, "%Y%m%d").month
    ```

```
months, sun_hours, rain_hours = np.loadtxt(sys.argv[1],
   delimiter=',', usecols=(1, 18, 21), unpack=True,
   converters={1: to_month, 18: to_float, 21: to_float})
```

2. Before calculating the basic statistics for the precipitation duration, we will create masked arrays for the sunshine and rain duration. There is a minor detail to take care of. Low values of sunshine duration are written down as -1 for some reason. I decided to convert those values to 0. It might have been better to completely ignore them. The code is as follows:

```
# Measurements are in .1 hours
rain_hours = .1 * ma.masked_invalid(rain_hours)

#Get rid of -1 values
print "# -1 values Before", len(sun_hours[sun_hours == -1])
sun_hours[sun_hours == -1] = 0
print "# -1 values After", len(sun_hours[sun_hours == -1])
sun_hours = .1 * ma.masked_invalid(sun_hours)

print "# Rain hours values", len(rain_hours.compressed())
print "Min Rain hours ", rain_hours.min(), "Max Rain
   hours", rain_hours.max()
print "Average", rain_hours.mean(), "Std. Dev",
   rain_hours.std()
```

This prints the following output:

```
# -1 values Before 832
# -1 values After 0 # Rain hours values 30373
Min Rain hours 0.0
Max Rain hours 24.0
Average 1.65149639482
Std. Dev 2.78643269679
```

As expected, the rain duration can be between 0 and 24 hours (or a full day).

3. We can average the sunshine and precipitation duration values quite easily over months. First, we create a numerical range for months. Second, we find array indices corresponding to each month. Then, we use indices to select duration values. The code is as follows:

```
monthly_rain = []
monthly_sun = []
month_range = np.arange(int(months.min()), int(months.max()))

for month in month_range:
```

Chapter 3

```
    indices = np.where(month == months)
    monthly_rain.append(rain_hours[indices].mean())
    monthly_sun.append(sun_hours[indices].mean())
```

4. The number of dry days is quite high, so we will leave them out in the precipitation duration histogram. We will plot bar charts of the average monthly rain and sunshine durations. The `cal` module is used here to display abbreviated month names in the plot. The code is as follows:

```
plt.subplot(211)
plt.title("Precipitation Duration Histogram")
plt.hist(rain_hours[rain_hours > 0].compressed(), 200)

width = 0.42
ax = plt.subplot(212)
plt.title("Monthly Precipitation Duration")
plt.bar(month_range, monthly_rain, width, label='Rain
  Hours')
plt.bar(month_range + width, monthly_sun, width,
  color='red', label='Sun Hours')
plt.legend()
ax.set_xticklabels(cal.month_abbr[::2])
ax.set_ylabel('Hours')
plt.show()
```

This gives us the following exciting plots:

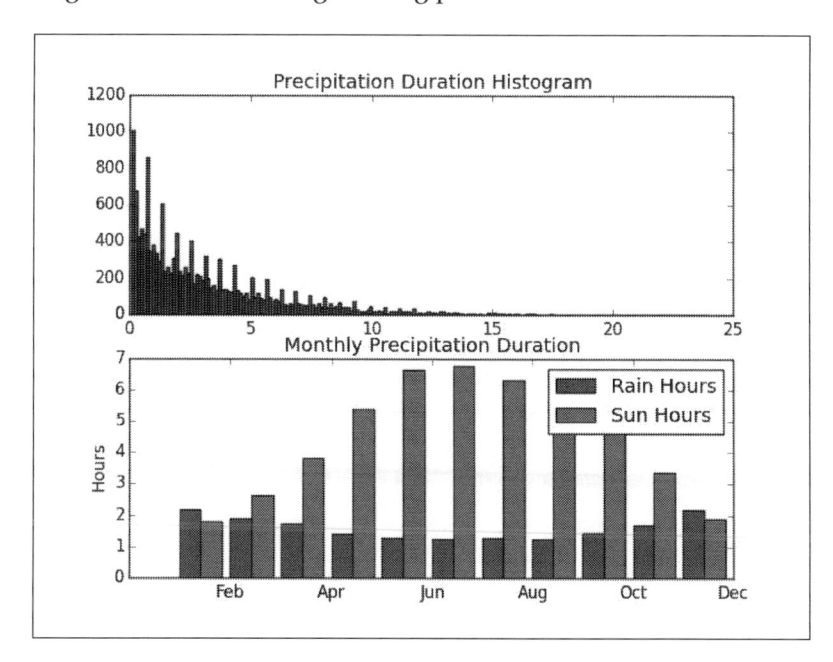

[65]

It seems that sunshine and precipitation duration are inversely correlated. So there must be an inverse correlation with temperatures based on the previous evidence in this series. We leave that as an exercise for readers to check. Obviously, the rain duration is limited between 0 and 24 hours, with lower values being much more likely. We can see clearly that in summer months the sun shines longer and it rains less (duration-wise). Similar conclusions can be drawn for other seasons.

Analyzing monthly precipitation in De Bilt

Let's take a look at the De Bilt precipitation data in 0.1 mm from KNMI. They are using the convention again of -1 representing low values. We are again going to set those values to 0:

1. We will load the dates converted to months, rain amounts, and rain duration in hours into NumPy arrays. Again, missing values needed to be converted to NaNs. We then create masked arrays for NumPy arrays with missing values. The code is as follows:

   ```
   to_float = lambda x: float(x.strip() or np.nan)
   to_month = lambda x: dt.strptime(x, "%Y%m%d").month
   months, duration, rain = np.loadtxt(sys.argv[1], delimiter=',',
   usecols=(1, 21, 22), unpack=True, converters={1: to_month, 21: to_
   float, 22: to_float})

   # Remove -1 values
   rain[rain == -1] = 0

   # Measurements are in .1 mm
   rain = .1 * ma.masked_invalid(rain)

   # Measurements are in .1 hours
   duration = .1 * ma.masked_invalid(duration)
   ```

2. We can calculate some simple statistics, such as minimum, maximum, mean, standard deviation, and correlation with precipitation duration. The last part is a bit tricky, because we need to match valid values. The values for a certain date of both precipitation and precipitation duration have to be valid. Luckily, this is pretty easy if we define a Boolean condition for masks of the arrays. The code is as follows:

   ```
   print "# Rain values", len(rain.compressed())
   print "Min Rain mm ", rain.min(), "Max Rain mm", rain.max()
   print "Average", rain.mean(), "Std. Dev", rain.std()

   mask = ~duration.mask & ~rain.mask
   ```

```
print "Correlation with duration",
   np.corrcoef(duration[mask], rain[mask])[0][1]
```

The previous code snippet prints the following values:

```
# Rain values 39139
Min Rain mm 0.0
Max Rain mm 62.3
Average 2.17747770766
Std. Dev 4.33715191714
Correlation with duration 0.779006349536
```

The correlation of the precipitation quantity with the duration of rain is not very strong, but still, it is the strongest correlation we have seen in this series so far. The author is convinced that both variables have been measured independently unlike sunshine duration, which is derived from global radiation.

Analyzing atmospheric pressure in De Bilt

Atmospheric pressure is the pressure exerted by air in the atmosphere. It is defined as force divided by area. The KNMI De Bilt data file has measurements in 0.1 hPa for average, minimum, and maximum daily pressures. We will plot a histogram of the average pressure and monthly minimums, maximums, and averages:

1. We will load the dates converted to months, average, minimum, and maximum pressure into NumPy arrays. Again, missing values needed to be converted to NaNs. The code is as follows:

    ```
    to_float = lambda x: 0.1 * float(x.strip() or np.nan)
    to_month = lambda x: dt.strptime(x, "%Y%m%d").month
    months, avg_p, max_p, min_p = np.loadtxt(sys.argv[1],
       delimiter=',', usecols=(1, 25, 26, 28), unpack=True,
       converters={1: to_month, 25: to_float, 26: to_float, 28:
       to_float})
    ```

2. Values are missing from the pressure value columns, so we have to create masked arrays out of NumPy arrays. The following code snippet prints some simple statistics:

    ```
    max_p = ma.masked_invalid(max_p)
    print "Maximum Pressure", max_p.max()

    avg_p = ma.masked_invalid(avg_p)
    ```

Basic Data Analysis with NumPy

```
print "Average Pressure", avg_p.mean(), "Std Dev", avg_p.std()

min_p = ma.masked_invalid(min_p)
print "Minimum Pressure", min_p.max()
```

This code snippet prints the following values:

Maximum Pressure 1050.4

Average Pressure 1015.14058231 Std Dev 9.85889134337

Minimum Pressure 1045.1

3. You can compute monthly averages, minimums, and maximums with the following code:

```
monthly_pressure = []
maxes = []
mins = []
month_range = np.arange(int(months.min()), int(months.max()))

for month in month_range:
    indices = np.where(month == months)
    monthly_pressure.append(avg_p[indices].mean())
    maxes.append(max_p[indices].max())
    mins.append(min_p[indices].min())
```

4. We will draw a histogram of the average daily pressures and the associated Gaussian curve. In addition, we will plot monthly aggregate values as prepared in the previous step. The code is as follows:

```
plt.subplot(211)
plt.title("Pressure Histogram")
a, bins, b = plt.hist(avg_p.compressed(), 200, normed=True)
stdev = avg_p.std()
avg = avg_p.mean()
plt.plot(bins, 1/(stdev * np.sqrt(2 * np.pi)) * np.exp(-
   (bins - avg)**2/(2 * stdev**2)), 'r-')

ax = plt.subplot(212)
plt.title("Monthly Pressure")
plt.plot(month_range, monthly_pressure, 'bo',
   label="Average")
plt.plot(month_range, maxes, 'r^', label="Maximum Values")
plt.plot(month_range, mins, 'g>', label="Minimum Values")
ax.set_xticklabels(cal.month_abbr[::2])
plt.legend(prop={'size':'x-small'}, loc='best')
ax.set_ylabel('hPa')
plt.show()
```

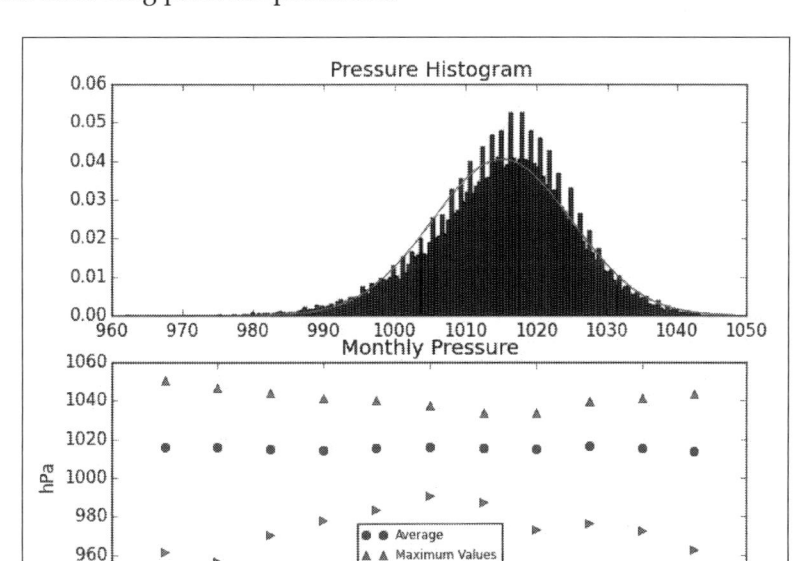

The following plots are produced:

As you can see, the bell curve fits the distribution of average daily pressures almost perfectly. The monthly average pressure seems to be constant.

Analyzing atmospheric humidity in De Bilt

Relative atmospheric humidity is the percentage of partial water vapor pressure of the maximum pressure at the same temperature in the atmosphere. During the summer months, high humidity can lead to issues with getting rid of excess heat by sweating. Humidity is also related to rain, dew, and fog. The KNMI De Bilt data file provides data on daily relative average, minimum, and maximum humidity in percentages. We will draw a histogram of the daily relative average humidity and monthly chart:

1. We will load the dates converted to months, daily relative average humidity, and the minimum and maximum humidity into NumPy arrays. Again, missing values needed to be converted into NaNs:

    ```
    to_float = lambda x: float(x.strip() or np.nan)
    to_month = lambda x: dt.strptime(x, "%Y%m%d").month
    months, avg_h, max_h, min_h = np.loadtxt(sys.argv[1],
       delimiter=',', usecols=(1, 35, 36, 38), unpack=True,
       converters={1: to_month, 35: to_float, 36: to_float, 38:
       to_float})
    ```

2. Values are missing from the relative humidity value columns, so we have to create masked arrays out of NumPy arrays. The following code snippet prints some simple statistics:

```
max_h = ma.masked_invalid(max_h)
print "Maximum Humidity", max_h.max()

avg_h = ma.masked_invalid(avg_h)
print "Average Humidity", avg_h.mean(), "Std Dev", avg_h.std()

min_h = ma.masked_invalid(min_h)
print "Minimum Humidity", min_h.min()
```

The statistics printed are as follows:

Maximum Humidity 111.0

Average Humidity 81.6147091109 Std Dev 10.3747295063

Minimum Humidity 8.0

The maximum relative humidity is above 100, which is kind of odd. We will draw a histogram of the relative average daily humidity. In addition, we will plot monthly aggregate values (refer to the atmospheric_humidity.py file in the Chapter03 folder of this book's code bundle). We will get the following plots as a result:

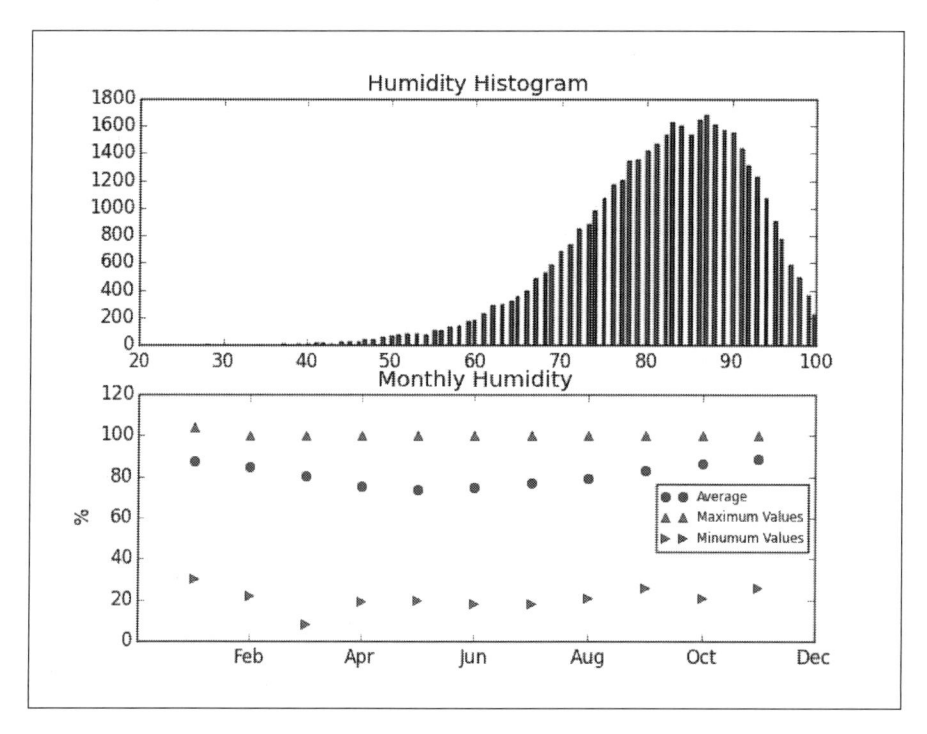

Something strange is going on with the maximum values. They seem to be above 100 percent. Maybe the author misunderstood the definition of relative humidity. However, the relative average humidity values seem to be between 0 and 100 percent as expected.

Summary

This chapter explained a great number of common NumPy functions. We explored the data from a KNMI weather station. The exploration is not exhaustive, so I encourage you to play with the data on your own. You should have realized by now how easy it is to do basic data analysis with NumPy and related Python libraries.

In the next chapter, we will go a step further and try to predict temperature using the same data.

4
Simple Predictive Analytics with NumPy

Following the exploration of the meteorological data in the previous chapter, we will now try to predict temperature. Usually, weather prediction is accomplished with complex models and top-of-the-line supercomputers. Most people don't have access to such resources, so we will cut corners and use simpler models. The list of topics covered in this chapter is as follows:

- Autocorrelation
- Autoregressive models
- Robust statistics

Examining autocorrelation of average temperature with pandas

The **pandas** (**Python data analysis**) library is just a collection of fancy wrappers around NumPy, Matplotlib, and other Python libraries. You can find more information including installation instructions on the pandas website at http://pandas.pydata.org/pandas-docs/stable/install.html. Most good APIs such as NumPy seem to follow the Unix philosophy—keep it simple and do one thing well. This philosophy results in many small tools and utilities that can be used as building blocks for something bigger. The pandas library mimics the R programming language in its approach.

Simple Predictive Analytics with NumPy

The pandas library has plotting subroutines, which can plot lag and autocorrelation plots. Autocorrelation is correlation within a dataset and can be indicative of a trend. For instance, if we have a lag of one day, we can see if the average temperature of yesterday influences the temperature today. For that to be the case, the autocorrelation value needs to be relatively high.

Pandas can also be used to resample data. Let's now learn how to resample the daily average temperature of the De Bilt data to give us annual averages.

In the following code snippets, `pd` refers to the imported pandas module. We will skip the imports and loading of data (for more details, see the `pandas_plots.py` file in the `Chapter04` folder of this book's code bundle). Let us now plot lagged data with the help of the following steps:

1. Create a `DatetimeIndex` object from a list of dates:

   ```
   dtidx = pd.DatetimeIndex([dt.fromordinal(int(date)) for
       date in dates])
   ```

2. Create a pandas `Series` array, which is a time series array. We have to multiply the temperatures by 0.1 because of the way temperatures are written down in the file:

   ```
   data = pd.Series(avg_temp * .1, index=dtidx)
   ```

3. Graph the lag plot as follows:

   ```
   lag_plot(data)
   ```

   The following lag plot is obtained, in which the next value `y(t+1)` in the time series is plotted against the previous value `y(t)`:

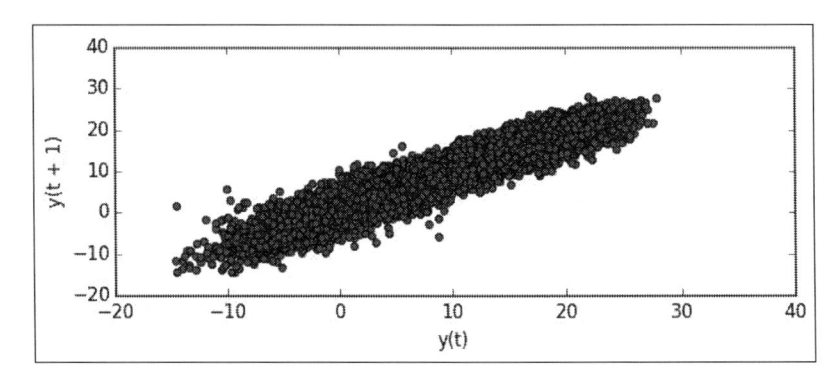

4. Plot the autocorrelation as follows:

   ```
   autocorrelation_plot(data)
   ```

[74]

This could result in the following chart:

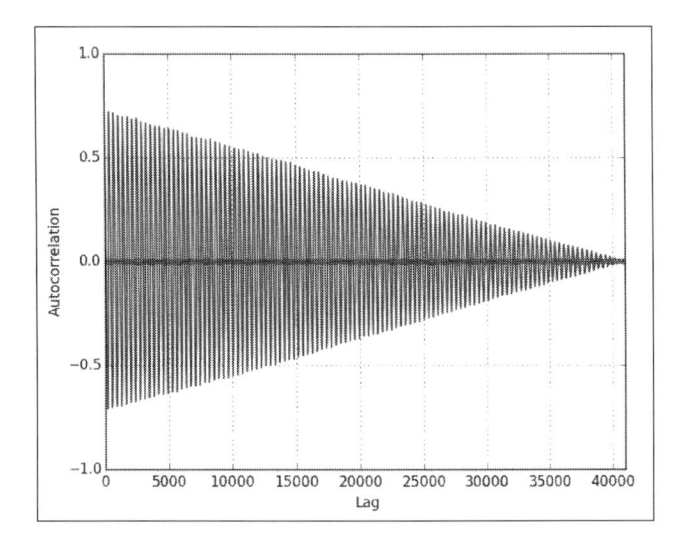

As you can see, the autocorrelation goes down with greater lag. This is important to remember for later.

5. Resample to annual (denoted by `'A'`) averages, and plot the resampled data as follows:

```
resampled = data.resample('A')
resampled.plot()
```

The resampled plot is shown as follows with the year against the average temperature:

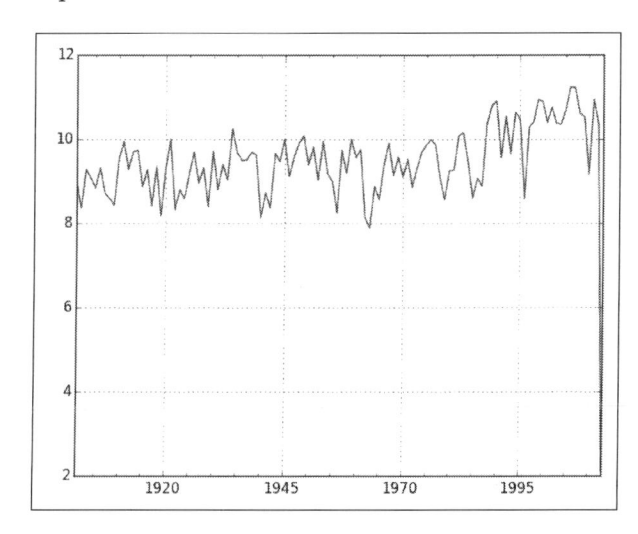

Simple Predictive Analytics with NumPy

You would have noticed that we did the same resampling in the previous chapter with plain NumPy, and it was a bit more work.

Describing data with pandas DataFrames

Luckily, pandas has descriptive statistics utilities. We will read the average wind speed, temperature, and pressure values from the KNMI De Bilt data file into a pandas DataFrame. This object is similar to the R dataframe, which is like a data table in a spreadsheet or a database. The columns are labeled, the data can be indexed, and you can run computations on the data. We will then print out descriptive statistics and a correlation matrix as shown in the following steps:

1. Read the CSV file with the pandas `read_csv` function. This function works in a similar fashion to the NumPy `load_txt` function:

   ```
   to_float = lambda x: .1 * float(x.strip() or np.nan)
   to_date = lambda x: dt.strptime(x, "%Y%m%d")
   cols = [4, 11, 25]
   conv_dict = dict( (col, to_float) for col in cols)

   conv_dict[1] = to_date
   cols.append(1)

   headers = ['dates', 'avg_ws', 'avg_temp', 'avg_pres']
   df = pd.read_csv(sys.argv[1], usecols=cols, names=headers,
      index_col=[0], converters=conv_dict)
   ```

2. Print the descriptive statistics with the functions described in the following table:

Function	Description
head	This is similar to the head Unix command and selects the first records of the DataFrame
tail	This is similar to the tail Unix command and selects the last records of the DataFrame
describe	This computes some predefined descriptive statistics
corr	This calculates the correlation matrix

   The code is as follows:

   ```
   print df.head()
   print

   print df.tail()
   ```

```
print

print df.describe()
print

print df.corr()
```

The output is as follows:

```
             avg_ws  avg_temp  avg_pres
dates
1901-01-01     NaN      -4.9       NaN
1901-01-02     NaN      -2.1       NaN
1901-01-03     NaN      -2.8       NaN
1901-01-04     NaN      -6.4       NaN
1901-01-05     NaN      -5.9       NaN

[5 rows x 3 columns]

             avg_ws  avg_temp  avg_pres
dates
2013-03-25     8.1       0.3    1015.9
2013-03-26     6.5       0.7    1014.4
2013-03-27     5.1       1.0    1012.2
2013-03-28     4.0       0.1    1010.7
2013-03-29     1.9      -0.4    1009.5

[5 rows x 3 columns]

              avg_ws      avg_temp       avg_pres
count   39871.000000  40996.000000  40631.000000
mean        4.221138      9.485723   1015.140582
std         1.939093      6.390069      9.859013
min         0.000000    -14.500000    962.100000
25%         2.700000      4.900000   1009.200000
50%         4.000000      9.600000   1015.800000
75%         5.100000     14.500000   1021.700000
max        16.500000     27.900000   1048.300000

[8 rows x 3 columns]

            avg_ws   avg_temp  avg_pres
avg_ws    1.000000  -0.126167 -0.368536
avg_temp -0.126167   1.000000 -0.037934
avg_pres -0.368536  -0.037934  1.000000
```

Correlating weather and stocks with pandas

We will try to correlate stock market data for the Netherlands with the DataFrame we produced last time from the KNMI De Bilt weather data. As a proxy for the stock market, we will use closing prices of the EWN ETF. This might not be the best choice, by the way, so if you have a better idea, please use the appropriate stock ticker. The steps for this exercise are provided as follows:

1. Download the EWN data from Yahoo Finance, with a special function. The code is as follows:

    ```
    #EWN start Mar 22, 1996
    start = dt(1996, 3, 22)
    end = dt(2013, 5, 4)

    symbol = "EWN"
    quotes = finance.quotes_historical_yahoo(symbol, start,
      end, asobject=True)
    ```

2. Create a `DataFrame` object with the available dates in the downloaded data:

    ```
    df2 = pd.DataFrame(quotes.close, index=dt_idx,
      columns=[symbol])
    ```

3. Join the new `DataFrame` object with `DataFrame` of the weather data. We will then obtain the correlation matrix:

    ```
    df3 = df.join(df2)

    print df3.corr()
    ```

    The correlation matrix is as follows:

	avg_ws	avg_temp	avg_pres	EWN
avg_ws	1.000000	-0.126167	-0.368536	0.033641
avg_temp	-0.126167	1.000000	-0.037934	0.018272
avg_pres	-0.368536	-0.037934	1.000000	-0.024083
EWN	0.033641	0.018272	-0.024083	1.000000

As you can observe, the correlation between stock price and weather parameters is quite weak.

Predicting temperature

Temperature is a thermodynamic variable, which quantifies being hot or cold. To predict temperature, we can apply our knowledge of thermodynamics and meteorology. This in general would result in the creation of complex weather models with a multitude of inputs. However, this is beyond the scope of this book, so we will try to keep our continuing example simple and manageable.

Autoregressive model with lag 1

What will the temperature be tomorrow? Probably, the same as today but a bit different. We can assume that temperature is a function of the temperature of the preceding day. This can be justified with the autocorrelation plot that we created earlier. To keep it simple, we will assume further that the function is a polynomial. We will define a cutoff point to be used for the fit. Ninety percent of the data should be used for that purpose. Let's model this idea with NumPy:

1. Fit the data to polynomials of different degrees with the `polyfit` function as shown in the following line of code:

   ```
   poly = np.polyfit( avg_temp[: cutoff - 1], avg_temp[1 :
     cutoff], degree)
   ```

2. Compute values based on the polynomial obtained in the previous step. Here, we use the remaining 10 percent of the data. The code is as follows:

   ```
   fit = np.polyval(poly, avg_temp[cutoff:-1])
   ```

3. Calculate the absolute difference between the actual temperature and the predicted temperatures:

   ```
   delta = np.abs(avg_temp[cutoff + 1:] - fit)
   ```

4. For each polynomial fit, the calculated percentage of deltas is within 1, 2, or 3 degrees Celsius error range, as shown in the following screenshot:

```
[ 0.94809073  0.48728787]
# % < 1 degree delta 38.9363259332
# % < 2 degree delta 68.2849475482
# % < 3 degree delta 86.655281776
[ 2.66746107e-04  9.43455438e-01   4.96431406e-01]
# % < 1 degree delta 38.9363259332
# % < 2 degree delta 68.260551354
# % < 3 degree delta 86.6796779702
[ -3.85275007e-04  9.41184196e-03  9.12326268e-01  3.49071070e-01]
# % < 1 degree delta 38.9363259332
# % < 2 degree delta 68.6508904611
# % < 3 degree delta 86.9236399122
```

As you can see, higher order polynomials give almost the same accuracy as the first-degree polynomial.

Autoregressive model with lag 2

Looking back two days, in theory, could make our model more accurate. Although, this is not guaranteed since the autocorrelation associated with lag 2 is not that strong. In NumPy, we have several ways to set up the model. Here I chose to do it with the `lstsq` function. We assume some kind of linear combination for the lag 1 and lag 2 components, and then apply linear regression. The method can be extended for a longer look-back period, but it probably is enough to stick to lag 2 for now. The steps for this exercise are provided as follows:

1. Set up a matrix A, and put in it the values for lags 2 and 1 up to the cutoff point. The code is as follows:

   ```
   A = np.zeros((2, cutoff - 2), float)

   A[0, ] = temp[:cutoff - 2]
   A[1, ] = temp[1 :cutoff - 1]
   ```

2. Create a vector b with the values we want to fit to:

   ```
   b = temp[2 : cutoff]
   ```

3. Solve the equation $Ax = b$. The code is as follows:

   ```
   (x, residuals, rank, s) = np.linalg.lstsq(A.T, b)
   print x
   ```

   The coefficients for lags 1 and 2 are printed as follows:

   ```
   [-0.08293789  1.06517683]
   ```

4. Predict values above the cutoff point:

   ```
   fit = x[0] * temp[cutoff-1:-2] + x[1] * temp[cutoff:-1]
   ```

5. Calculate the absolute errors:

   ```
   delta = np.abs(temp[cutoff + 1:] - fit)
   ```

6. Plot a histogram of the absolute errors:

   ```
   plt.hist(delta, bins = 10, normed=True)
   ```

The histogram for the absolute error is given as follows (refer to the `lag2.py` file in the `Chapter04` folder of this book's code bundle):

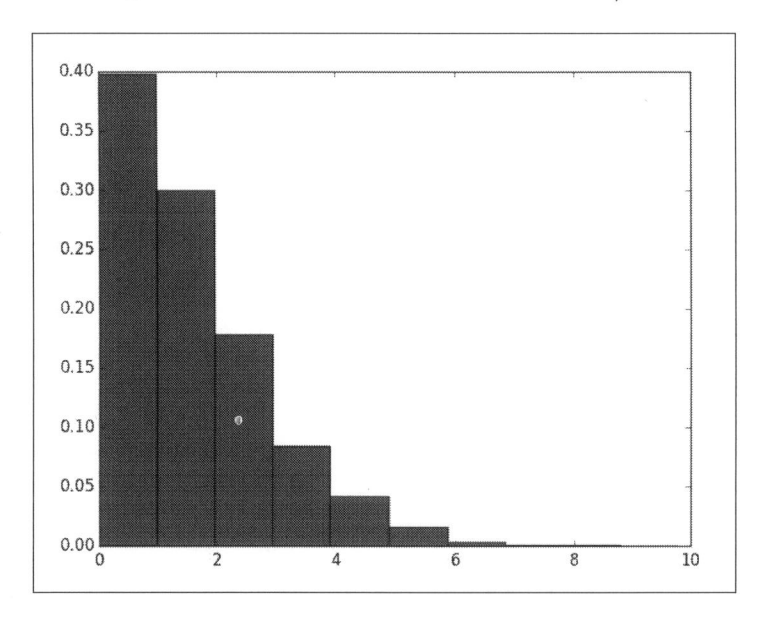

Analyzing intra-year daily average temperatures

We are going to have a look at the temperature variation within a year by converting dates to the corresponding day of the year in numbers. This number is between 1 and 366, where 1 corresponds to January 1st and 365 (or 366) corresponds to December 31st. Perform the following steps to analyze the intra-year daily average temperature:

1. Initialize arrays for the range 1-366 with averages initialized to `zeros`:

   ```
   rng = np.arange(1, 366)
   avgs = np.zeros(365)
   avgs2 = np.zeros(365)
   ```

2. Calculate averages by the day of the year before and after a cutoff point:

   ```
   for i in rng:
       indices = np.where(days[:cutoff] == i)
       avgs[i-1] = temp[indices].mean()
       indices = np.where(days[cutoff+1:] == i)
       avgs2[i-1] = temp[indices].mean()
   ```

Simple Predictive Analytics with NumPy

3. Fit the averages before the cutoff point to a quadratic polynomial (just a first-order approximation):

   ```
   poly = np.polyfit(rng, avgs, 2)
   print poly
   ```

   The following polynomial coefficients in descending power are printed:

   ```
   [ -4.91329859e-04   1.92787493e-01   -3.98075418e+00]
   ```

4. Plot the average after the cutoff point, and display a fit using the polynomial we obtained:

   ```
   plt.plot(avgs2)
   plt.plot(np.polyval(poly, rng))
   plt.show()
   ```

   As you can see in the following plot, the fit is pretty good but not perfect. In the middle of the year, as you can observe around summer, we have peak temperatures. In January and December, the temperature hits bottom.

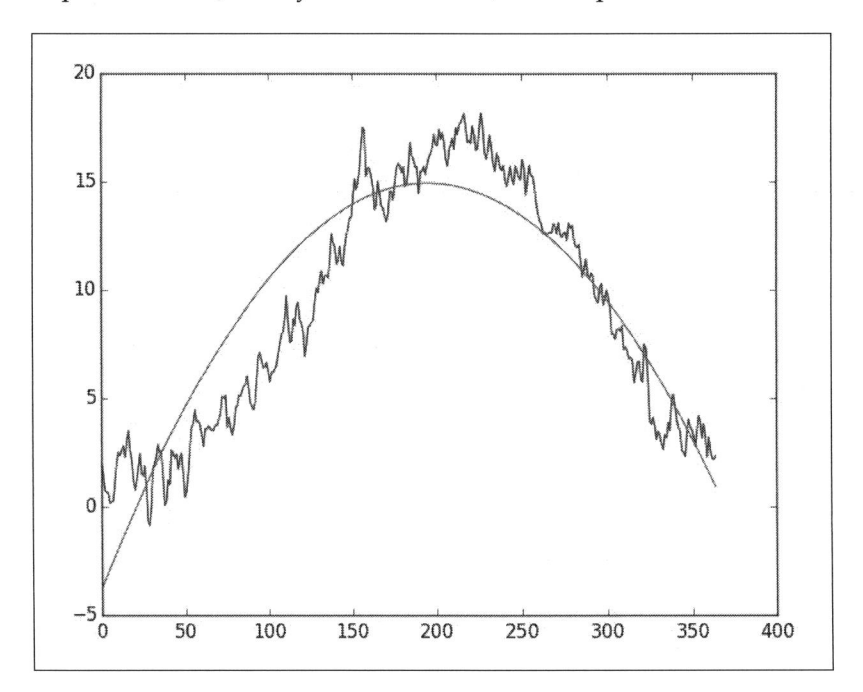

Introducing the day-of-the-year temperature model

Continuing with the work we did in the previous example, I would like to propose a new model, where temperature is a function of the day of the year (between 1 and 366). Of course, this model is not complete, but can be used as a component in a more advanced model, which should take into account the previous autoregressive model that we did with lag 2. The procedure for this model is illustrated as follows:

1. Fit the temperature data before the cutoff point to a quadratic polynomial just as in the previous section but without averaging:

   ```
   poly = np.polyfit(days[:cutoff], temp[:cutoff], 2)
   print poly
   ```

   Believe it or not, we get the same polynomial coefficients we got earlier:

   ```
   [ -4.91072584e-04   1.92682505e-01  -3.97182941e+00]
   ```

2. Calculate the absolute difference between the predicted and actual values:

   ```
   delta = np.abs(np.polyval(poly, days[cutoff:]) -
      temp[cutoff:])
   ```

3. Plot a histogram of the absolute error:

   ```
   plt.hist(delta, bins = 10, normed = True)
   plt.show()
   ```

   Refer to the following plot. It seems that we got a better result with the autoregressive model.

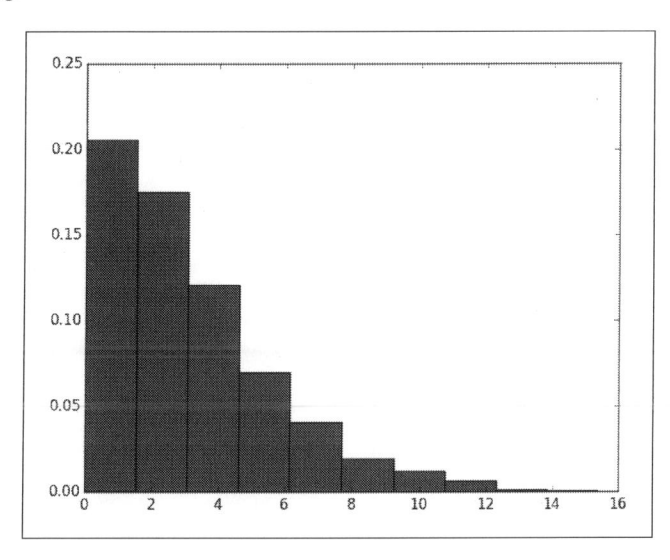

Modeling temperature with the SciPy leastsq function

So, now we have two ideas: either the temperature today depends on the temperature yesterday and the day before yesterday, and we assume that some kind of linear combination is formed, or the temperature depends on a day of the year (between 1 and 366). We can combine these ideas, but then the question is how. It seems that we could have a multiplicative model or an additive model.

Let's choose the additive model since it seems simpler. This means that we assume that temperature is the sum of the autoregressive component and a cyclical component. It's easy to write this down into one equation. We will use the SciPy `leastsq` function to minimize the square of the error of this equation. The procedure for this model is illustrated as follows:

1. Define a function that computes the error of our model. The code is as follows:
   ```
   def error(p, d, t, lag2, lag1):
      l2, l1, d2, d1, d0 = p

      return t - l2 * lag2 + l1 * lag1 + d2 * d ** 2 + d1 * d + d0
   ```

2. Give an initial guess for all the parameters in our equation:
   ```
   p0 = [-0.08293789,   1.06517683, -4.91072584e-04,
      1.92682505e-01,  -3.97182941e+00]
   ```

   The values here come from the previous programs, but in principle you could use other values as long as the solution converges sufficiently fast.

3. Apply the `leastsq` function as shown in the following lines of code:
   ```
   params = leastsq(error, p0, args=(days[2:cutoff],
      temp[2:cutoff], temp[:cutoff - 2], temp[1 :cutoff -
      1]))[0]
   print params
   ```

4. The final parameters of the model are printed as follows. It looks like all parameters except the first one have decreased in absolute size. I don't know if that's coincidental, but as far as I know, the order of the parameters shouldn't matter.
   ```
   [ -1.52297691e-01   -9.89195783e-01    8.20879954e-05   -
      3.16870659e-02    6.06397834e-01]
   ```

5. We then calculate the absolute error for the model applied above the cutoff point and plot the histogram of the error. The code is omitted here for the sake of brevity.

   Refer to the following plot. The accuracy of the model doesn't seem to be better than the simple autoregressive model with lag 2.

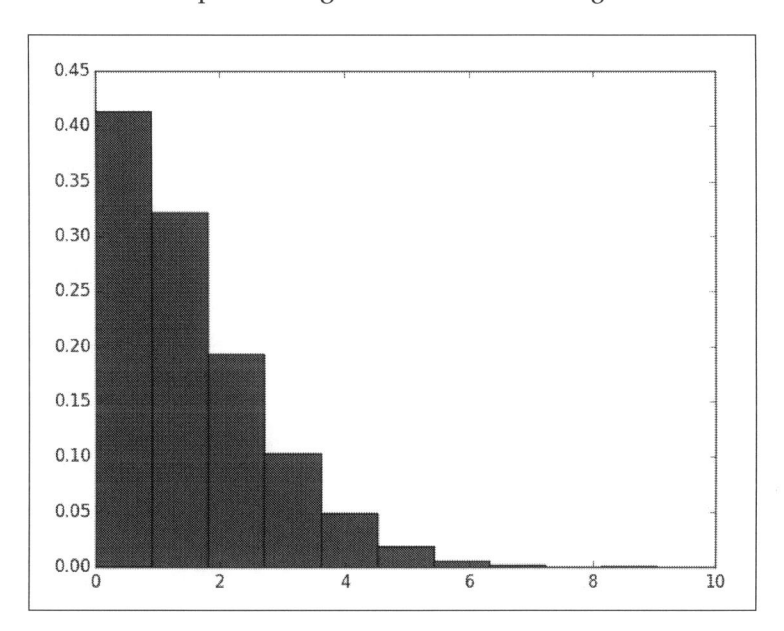

Day-of-year temperature take two

The quadratic polynomial approximation for the day-of-the-year temperature fit can be improved upon. We haven't used any of the NumPy trigonometric functions until now. Those should be a good fit for this problem. So, let's try a trigonometric function and fit again using a function from the `scipy.optimize` module (`leastsq` to be precise) as follows:

1. Set up a simple `model` function and an `error` function to be minimized, as shown in the following code snippet:

   ```
   def model(p, d):
       a, b, w, c = p
       return a + b * np.cos(w * d + c)

   def error(p, d, t):
       return t - model(p, d)
   ```

2. Give the initial guess and fit the data:

   ```
   p0 = [.1, 1, .01, .01]
   params = leastsq(error, p0, args=(days, temp))[0]
   print params
   ```

   We get the following parameters:

   ```
   [ 9.6848106  -7.59870042 -0.01766333 -5.83349705]
   ```

   > Here, -2 *pi* over 365 is equal to the third parameter. I believe that the first parameter is equal to the average of all the temperatures, and we can come up with similar explanations for the other parameters. Calculate averages for each day of the year and plot averages and fitted values. We have done this before, so this part of the code is omitted.

We get the fit in the following chart:

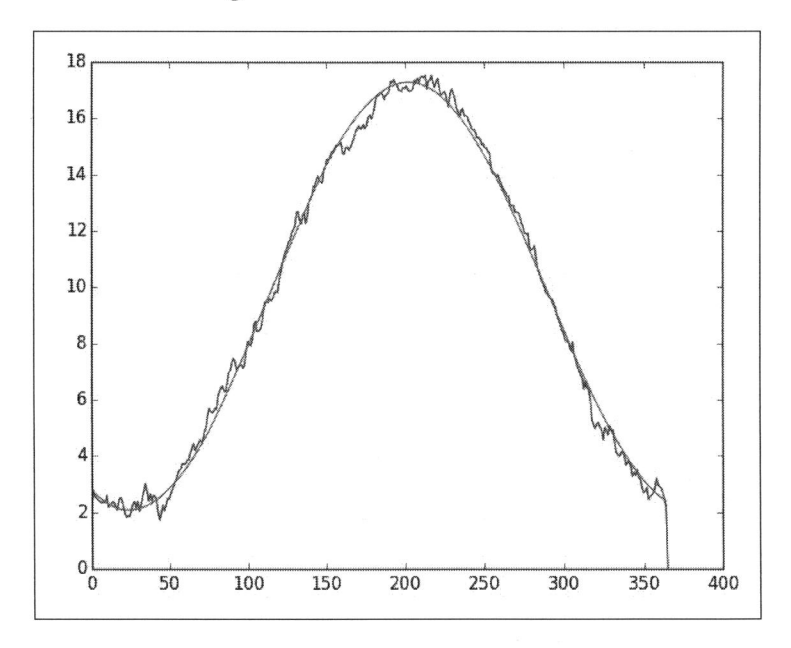

Moving-average temperature model with lag 1

The moving average model of a time series represents the data as oscillations around the mean of the data. It is assumed that the lag components are white noise (not a politically incorrect term as far as I know), which forms a linear combination. We will again use the `leastsq` function to fit a model:

1. We will start off with a simple moving-average model. It has only one lag component and therefore only one coefficient. The code snippet is as follows:

    ```
    def model(p, ma1):
       return p * ma1
    ```

2. Call the `leastsq` function. Here, we subtract the mean from the data:

    ```
    params = leastsq(error, p0, args=(temp[1:cutoff] - mu,
       temp[:cutoff-1] - mu))[0]
    print params
    ```

    The program prints the following parameter:

    `[ 0.94809073]`

    We get the following plot for the absolute error histogram, which is comparable to the autoregressive model results:

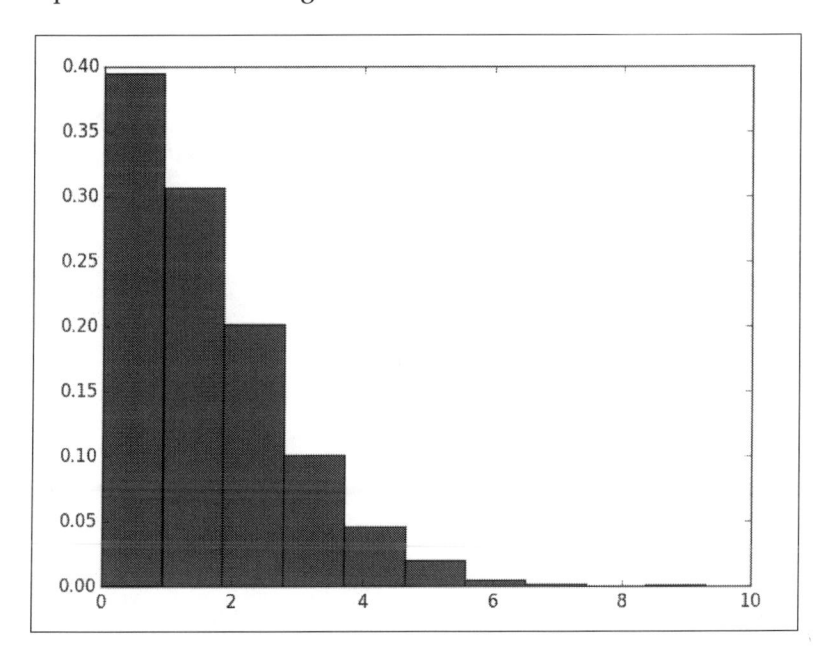

Simple Predictive Analytics with NumPy

The Autoregressive Moving Average temperature model

The **Autoregressive Moving Average (ARMA)** model mixes the **Autoregressive (AR)** and **Moving Average (MA)** models. We have already discussed both models. Informally, we can say that we have the autoregressive component with white noise around it. Part of this white noise can be modeled as a linear combination of lag components plus some constant as follows:

1. Define an autoregressive model with lag 2 using linear coefficients we obtained with a previous script:

    ```
    def ar(a):
        ar_p = [1.06517683, -0.08293789]

        return ar_p[0] * a[1:-1] + ar_p[1] * a[:-2]
    ```

2. Define the moving average model with lag 1:

    ```
    def model(p, ma1):
        c0, c1 = p

        return c0 + c1 * ma1
    ```

3. Subtract the autoregressive model values from the data, giving us the error terms (white noise):

    ```
    err_terms = temp[cutoff+1:] - ar(temp[cutoff-1:])
    ```

    Most of the code for this model should appear familiar to you as shown in the following code:

    ```
    import sys
    import numpy as np
    import matplotlib.pyplot as plt
    from datetime import datetime as dt
    from scipy.optimize import leastsq

    temp = .1 * np.loadtxt(sys.argv[1], delimiter=',',
        usecols=(11,), unpack=True)
    cutoff = 0.9 * len(temp)

    def model(p, ma1):
    ```

```
        c0, c1 = p

        return c0 + c1 * ma1

    def error(p, t, ma1):
        return t - model(p, ma1)

    p0 = [.1, .1]

    def ar(a):
        ar_p = [1.06517683, -0.08293789]

        return ar_p[0] * a[1:-1] + ar_p[1] * a[:-2]

    err_terms = temp[2:cutoff] - ar(temp[:cutoff])
    params = leastsq(error, p0, args=(err_terms[1:],
       err_terms[:-1]))[0]
    print params

    err_terms = temp[cutoff+1:] - ar(temp[cutoff-1:])
    delta = np.abs(error(params, err_terms[1:], err_terms[:-
       1]))
    print "% delta less than 2", (100. * len(delta[delta <=
       2]))/len(delta)

    plt.hist(delta, bins = 10, normed = True)
    plt.show()
```

The output of the script is as follows:

```
[ 0.16506278  0.01041355]
% delta less than 2 69.7169350903
```

The time-dependent temperature mean adjusted autoregressive model

It's a mouthful, but it's not nearly as complicated as it sounds. Let's parse the title in the following points:

- As we found out, the average temperature for each day of the year seems to fit an annual cycle. It may have to do with the rotation of the Earth around the Sun.

Simple Predictive Analytics with NumPy

- There appears to be a trend of increasing temperature. Some have called that global warming and blame industry and human beings in general for it. Without getting into a political discussion, let's assume that there is truth in this claim. Further, let's assume for now that this trend depends on the year. I know I will get into trouble for this, but let's also assume for now that the relation is based on a first-degree polynomial (a straight line).
- For the sake of argument, let's claim that the previous two points together form a time-dependent mean. We will model what is left over as a linear combination of autoregressive lag components.

We need to perform the following steps to set up and create the model:

1. Create arrays for the day of the year, years, and temperature.
2. Average the temperature for each day of the year.
3. Subtract the day-of-the-year average values from the values in the previous step.
4. Fit the remainder to a straight line and subtract the fit from the remainder.
5. Do a least squares fit to an autoregressive model with lag 2.

    Predict the temperature according to this model and plot the absolute error.

The code is straightforward and given as follows:

```
import sys
import numpy as np
import matplotlib.pyplot as plt
from datetime import datetime as dt
from scipy.optimize import leastsq

to_ordinal = lambda x: dt.strptime(x, "%Y%m%d").toordinal()
ordinals, temp = np.loadtxt(sys.argv[1], delimiter=',', usecols=(1, 11), unpack=True, converters={1: to_ordinal})
days = np.array([dt.fromordinal(int(d)).timetuple().tm_yday for d in ordinals])
years = np.array([dt.fromordinal(int(d)).year for d in ordinals])
temp = .1 * temp
cutoff = 0.9 * len(temp)

avgs = np.zeros(366)

for i in xrange(1, 366):
    indices = np.where(days[:cutoff] == i)
```

```python
    avgs[i-1] = temp[indices].mean()

def subtract_avgs(a, doy):
    return a - avgs[doy.astype(int)-1]

def subtract_trend(a, poly, b):
    return a - poly[0] * b - poly[1]

def print_stats(a):
    print "Min", a.min(), "Max", a.max(), "Mean", a.mean(), "Std", a.std()
    print

# Step 1. DOY avgs
less_avgs = subtract_avgs(temp[:cutoff], days[:cutoff])
print "After Subtracting DOY avgs"
print_stats(less_avgs)

# Step 2. Linear trend
trend = np.polyfit(years[:cutoff], less_avgs, 1)
print "Trend coeff", trend
less_trend = subtract_trend(less_avgs, trend, years[:cutoff])
print "After Subtracting Linear Trend"
print_stats(less_trend)

def model(p, lag2, lag1):
    l1, l2 = p

    return l2 * lag2 + l1 * lag1

def error(p, t, lag2, lag1):
    return t - model(p, lag2, lag1)

p0 = [1.06517683, -0.08293789]
params = leastsq(error, p0, args=(less_trend[2:], less_trend[:-2], less_trend[1:-1]))[0]
print "AR params", params

#Step 1. again
less_avgs = subtract_avgs(temp[cutoff+1:], days[cutoff+1:])

#Step 2. again
```

Simple Predictive Analytics with NumPy

```
less_trend = subtract_trend(less_avgs, trend, years[cutoff+1:])

delta = np.abs(error(params, less_trend[2:], less_trend[:-2], less_trend[1:-1]))
print "% delta less than 2", (100. * len(delta[delta <= 2]))/len(delta)

plt.hist(delta, bins = 10, normed = True)
plt.show()
```

The following output is printed:

```
After Subtracting DOY avgs
Min -16.6386138614 Max 12.0485148515 Mean 0.000775151777971 Std 3.34256572221

Trend coeff [  1.00962465e-02  -1.96970923e+01]
After Subtracting Linear Trend
Min -16.6897796704 Max 12.0882152606 Mean -1.02687291069e-12 Std 3.32957560366

AR params [ 0.96123255 -0.18460592]
% delta less than 2 71.5889675372
```

Outliers analysis of average De Bilt temperature

Outliers are values in a dataset that are to be considered extreme. Outliers can be caused by measurement or other types of errors, or they could be caused by a natural phenomenon. There are several definitions for outliers. In this example, we will be using the definition for mild outliers. This definition depends on the position of the first and the third quartiles. A quarter and three quarters of the items in the dataset are smaller than the first and third quartile values, respectively. The difference between these specific quartiles is called the **inter-quartile range**. It's a robust measure for dispersion similar to standard deviation. Mild outliers are defined to be 1.5 inter-quartile ranges away from either the first or third quartile. We can study the temperature outliers as follows:

1. Find the first quartile with a function from SciPy:

    ```
    q1 = scoreatpercentile(temp, 25)
    ```

2. Find the third quartile:

    ```
    q3 = scoreatpercentile(temp, 75)
    ```

3. Find the indices of the mild outliers:

    ```
    indices = np.where(temp < (q1 - N * irq))
    ```

Chapter 4

4. Plot the differences of the indices (showing clustering) and the outliers:

```
plt.subplot(211)
plt.plot(np.diff(indices)[0])
plt.title('Indices Diff')
plt.subplot(212)
plt.title('Outliers Temperature')
plt.plot(outliers)
plt.show()
```

The following NumPy code analyzes outliers and tries to find out whether any clustering of outliers occurs:

```
import sys
import numpy as np
import matplotlib.pyplot as plt
from scipy.stats import scoreatpercentile
from datetime import datetime as dt

to_ordinal = lambda x: dt.strptime(x, "%Y%m%d").toordinal()
ordinals, temp = np.loadtxt(sys.argv[1], delimiter=',', usecols=(1,
11), unpack=True, converters={1: to_ordinal})
temp = .1 * temp
q1 = scoreatpercentile(temp, 25)
print "1st Quartile", q1
q3 = scoreatpercentile(temp, 75)
print "3rd Quartile", q3
irq = q3 - q1
print "Std", temp.std(), "IRQ", irq
N = 1.5
print len(temp[temp > (q3 + N * irq)])
indices = np.where(temp < (q1 - N * irq))

outliers =   temp[indices]
print "#Outliers", len(outliers)
plt.subplot(211)
plt.plot(np.diff(indices)[0])
plt.title('Indices Diff')
plt.subplot(212)
plt.title('Outliers Temperature')
plt.plot(outliers)
plt.show()
```

Simple Predictive Analytics with NumPy

It becomes clear that the outliers are on the colder side as shown in the following output:

```
1st Quartile 4.9
3rd Quartile 14.5
Std 6.38999133865 IRQ 9.6
0
#Outliers 85
```

The following plot shows some clustering, but no regular pattern as far as I can see:

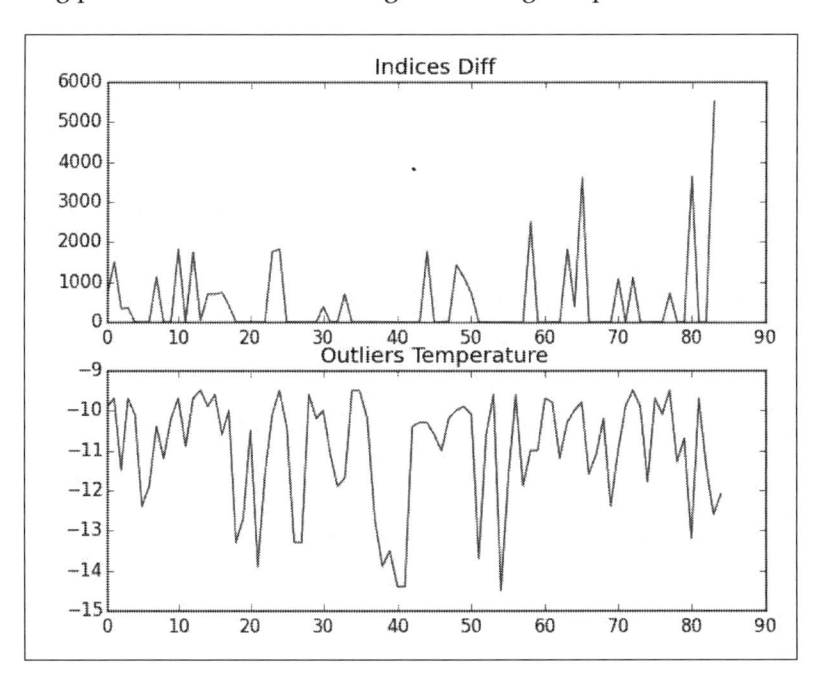

Using more robust statistics

We can make our code from the *The time-dependent temperature mean adjusted autoregressive model* section more robust by doing the following:

- Computing the median instead of the mean

    ```
    avgs[i-1] = np.median(temp[indices])
    ```

- Ignoring the outliers with a masked array

    ```
    temp[:cutoff] = ma.masked_array(temp[:cutoff],
      temp[:cutoff] < (q1 - 1.5 * irq))
    ```

[94]

We get slightly different output with the modified code, with about 70 percent of the values predicted having an absolute error of less than 2 degrees Celsius:

```
AR params [ 0.95095073 -0.17373633]
% delta less than 2 70.8567244325
```

Summary

In this chapter, we learned several simple techniques to predict temperature. Of course, they are not at the level of meteorologists who have access to supercomputers and can apply complex equations. But we did come pretty far with our simple approach.

In the next chapter, we will switch to different datasets. The next chapter will focus on signal processing techniques.

5
Signal Processing Techniques

We will learn about some signal-processing techniques in this chapter, and we will analyze time-series data with these. As example data, we will use the sunspot data provided by a Belgian scientific institute. We can download this data from several places on the Internet, and it is also provided as sample data by the statsmodels library. There are a number of things we can do with the data, such as:

- Trying to determine periodic cycles within the data. This can be done, but this is a bit advanced, so we will just get you started.
- Smoothing the data to filter out noise.
- Forecasting.

Introducing the Sunspot data

Sunspots are dark spots visible on the Sun's surface. This phenomenon has been studied for many centuries by astronomers. Evidence has been found for periodic sunspot cycles. We can download up-to-date annual sunspot data from http://www.quandl.com/SIDC/SUNSPOTS_A-Sunspot-Numbers-Annual. This is provided by the Belgian Solar Influences Data Analysis Center. The data goes back to 1700 and contains more than 300 annual averages. In order to determine sunspot cycles, scientists successfully used the *Hilbert-Huang* transform (refer to http://en.wikipedia.org/wiki/Hilbert%E2%80%93Huang_transform). A major part of this transform is the so-called **Empirical Mode Decomposition** (**EMD**) method. The entire algorithm contains many iterative steps, and we will cover only some of them here. EMD reduces data to a group of **Intrinsic Mode Functions** (**IMF**). You can compare this to the way Fast Fourier Transform decomposes a signal in a superposition of *sine* and *cosine* terms.

Signal Processing Techniques

Extracting IMFs is done via a sifting process. The sifting of a signal is related to separating out components of a signal one at a time. The first step of this process is identifying local extrema. We will perform the first step and plot the data with the extrema we found. Let's download the data in CSV format. In *Chapter 3, Basic Data Analysis with NumPy*, we learned how to load CSV files into NumPy arrays, so, if necessary, please go back to read up on that. We also need to reverse the array to have it in the correct chronological order (see *Chapter 2, NumPy Basics*, for details if needed). The following code snippet finds the indices of the local minima and maxima respectively:

```
mins = signal.argrelmin(data)[0]
maxs = signal.argrelmax(data)[0]
```

Now we need to concatenate these arrays and use the indices to select the corresponding values. The following code accomplishes that and also plots the data:

```
import numpy as np
import sys
import matplotlib.pyplot as plt
from scipy import signal

data = np.loadtxt(sys.argv[1], delimiter=',', usecols=(1,),
unpack=True, skiprows=1)
#reverse order
data = data[::-1]

mins = signal.argrelmin(data)[0]
maxs = signal.argrelmax(data)[0]
extrema = np.concatenate((mins, maxs))

year_range = np.arange(1700, 1700 + len(data))

plt.plot(1700 + extrema, data[extrema], 'go')
plt.plot(year_range, data)
plt.show()
```

We will see the following chart:

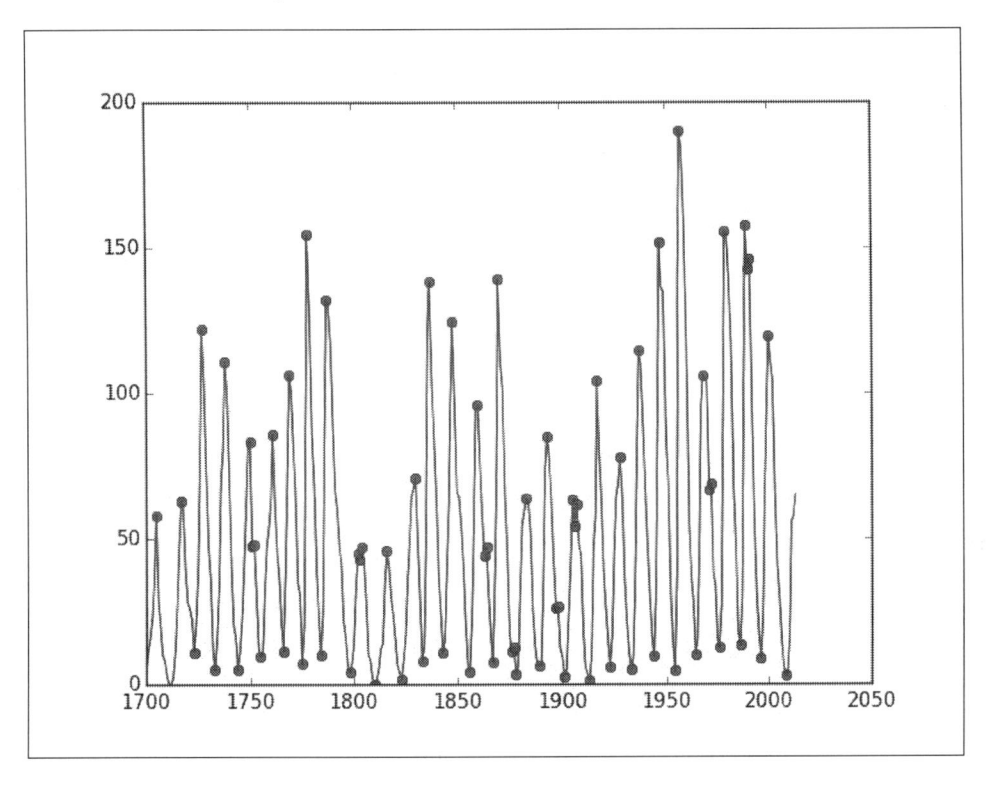

In this plot, you can see the extrema is indicated with dots.

Sifting continued

The next steps in the sifting process require us to interpolate with a cubic spline of the minima and maxima. This creates an upper envelope and a lower envelope, which should surround the data. The mean of the envelopes is needed for the next iteration of the EMD process. We can interpolate minima with the following code snippet:

```
spl_min = interpolate.interp1d(mins, data[mins], kind='cubic')
min_rng = np.arange(mins.min(), mins.max())
l_env = spl_min(min_rng)
```

Signal Processing Techniques

Similar code can be used to interpolate the maxima. We need to be aware that the interpolation results are only valid within the range over which we are interpolating. This range is defined by the first occurrence of a minima/maxima and ends at the last occurrence of a minima/maxima. Unfortunately, the interpolation ranges we can define in this way for the maxima and minima do not match perfectly. So, for the purpose of plotting, we need to extract a shorter range that lies within both the maxima and minima interpolation ranges. Have a look at the following code:

```
import numpy as np
import sys
import matplotlib.pyplot as plt
from scipy import signal
from scipy import interpolate

data = np.loadtxt(sys.argv[1], delimiter=',', usecols=(1,), unpack=True, skiprows=1)
#reverse order
data = data[::-1]

mins = signal.argrelmin(data)[0]
maxs = signal.argrelmax(data)[0]
extrema = np.concatenate((mins, maxs))

year_range = np.arange(1700, 1700 + len(data))
spl_min = interpolate.interp1d(mins, data[mins], kind='cubic')
min_rng = np.arange(mins.min(), mins.max())
l_env = spl_min(min_rng)

spl_max = interpolate.interp1d(maxs, data[maxs], kind='cubic')
max_rng = np.arange(maxs.min(), maxs.max())
u_env = spl_max(max_rng)

inclusive_rng = np.arange(max(min_rng[0], max_rng[0]), min(min_rng[-1], max_rng[-1]))
mid = (spl_max(inclusive_rng) + spl_min(inclusive_rng))/2

plt.plot(year_range, data)
plt.plot(1700 + min_rng, l_env, '-x')
plt.plot(1700 + max_rng, u_env, '-x')
plt.plot(1700 + inclusive_rng, mid, '--')
plt.show()
```

The code produces the following chart:

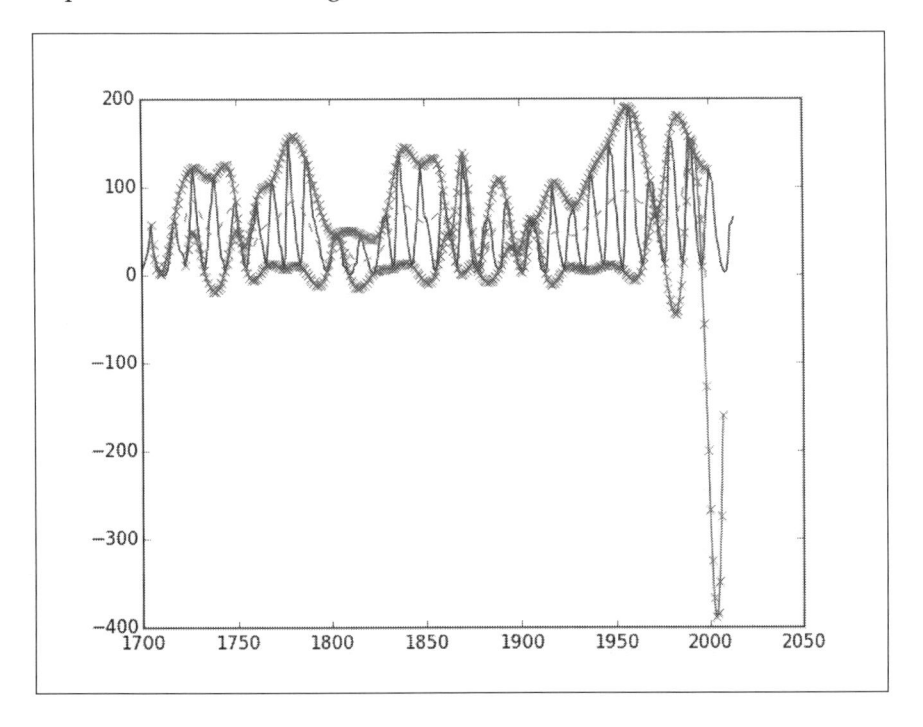

What you see is the observed data, with computed envelopes and *mid* line. Obviously, negative values don't make any sense in this context. However, for the algorithm we only need to care about the mid line of the upper and lower envelopes. In these first two sections, we basically performed the first iteration of the EMD process. The algorithm is a bit more involved, so we will leave it up to you whether or not you want to continue with this analysis on your own.

Moving averages

Moving averages are tools commonly used to analyze time-series data. A moving average defines a window of previously seen data that is averaged each time the window slides forward one period. The different types of moving average differ essentially in the weights used for averaging. The exponential moving average, for instance, has exponentially decreasing weights with time. This means that older values have less influence than newer values, which is sometimes desirable.

Signal Processing Techniques

We can express an equal-weight strategy for the simple moving average as follows in the NumPy code:

```
weights = np.exp(np.linspace(-1., 0., N))
weights /= weights.sum()
```

A simple moving average uses equal weights which, in code, looks as follows:

```
def sma(arr, n):
   weights = np.ones(n) / n

   return np.convolve(weights, arr)[n-1:-n+1]
```

The following code plots the simple moving average for the 11- and 22-year sunspot cycle:

```
import numpy as np
import sys
import matplotlib.pyplot as plt

data = np.loadtxt(sys.argv[1], delimiter=',', usecols=(1,),
unpack=True, skiprows=1)
#reverse order
data = data[::-1]

year_range = np.arange(1700, 1700 + len(data))

def sma(arr, n):
   weights = np.ones(n) / n

   return np.convolve(weights, arr)[n-1:-n+1]

sma11 = sma(data, 11)
sma22 = sma(data, 22)

plt.plot(year_range, data, label='Data')
plt.plot(year_range[10:], sma11, '-x', label='SMA 11')
plt.plot(year_range[21:], sma22, '--', label='SMA 22')
plt.legend()
plt.show()
```

In the following plot, we see the original data and the simple moving averages for 11- and 22-year periods. As you can see, moving averages are not a good fit for this data; this is generally the case for sinusoidal data.

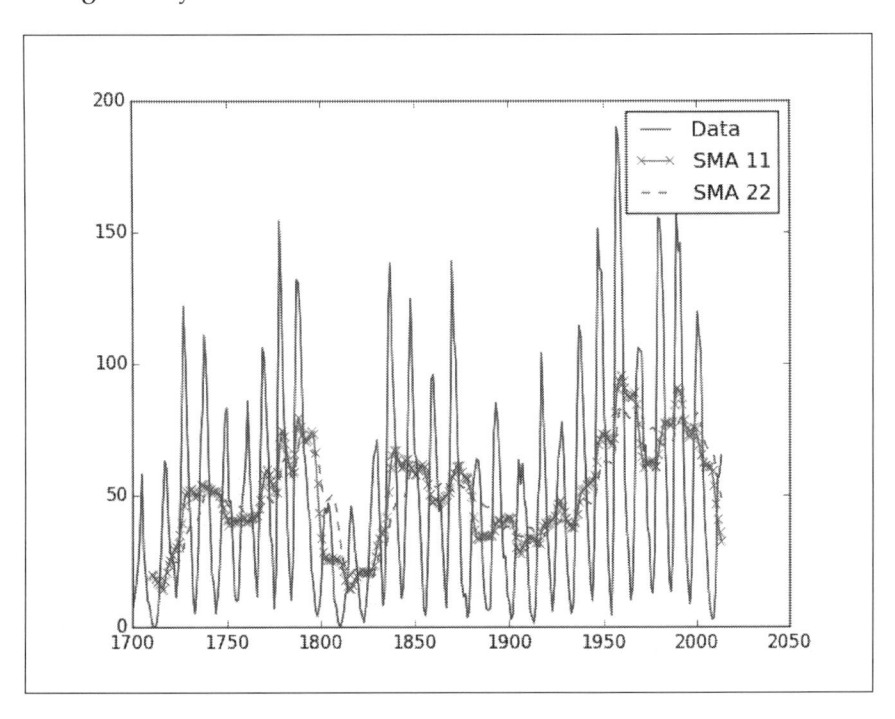

Smoothing functions

Smoothing can help us get rid of noise and outliers in raw data. This, for instance, makes it easier to spot trends in the data. NumPy provides a number of smoothing functions.

> These functions can calculate weights in a sliding window as we did in the previous example (for more background information, visit http://en.wikipedia.org/wiki/Window_function).

These functions, except the kaiser function, require only one parameter—the size of the window, which we will set to 22 for the middle cycle of the sunspot data. The kaiser function also needs a beta parameter. With this parameter, the kaiser function can mimic the other functions.

Signal Processing Techniques

The NumPy documentation recommends a starting value of 14 for the `beta` parameter, so that is what we are going to use too. The code is straightforward and given as follows (the data here is limited to the last 50 years only for easier comparison in the plots):

```
import numpy as np
import sys
import matplotlib.pyplot as plt

def smooth(weights, arr):
    return np.convolve(weights/weights.sum(), arr)

data = np.loadtxt(sys.argv[1], delimiter=',', usecols=(1,),
unpack=True, skiprows=1)
#reverse order
data = data[::-1]

#Select last 50 years
data = data[-50:]
year_range = np.arange(1963, 2013)
print len(data), len(year_range)

plt.plot(year_range, data, label="Data")
plt.plot(year_range, smooth(np.hanning(22), data)[21:], 'x',
label='Hanning 22')
plt.plot(year_range, smooth(np.bartlett(22), data)[21:], 'o',
label='Bartlett 22')
plt.plot(year_range, smooth(np.blackman(22), data)[21:], '--',
label='Blackman 22')
plt.plot(year_range, smooth(np.hamming(22), data)[21:], '^',
label='Hamming 22')
plt.plot(year_range, smooth(np.kaiser(22, 14), data)[21:], ':',
label='Kaiser 22')
plt.legend()
plt.show()
```

In the following plot, we can see that the result of the window functions doesn't differ much:

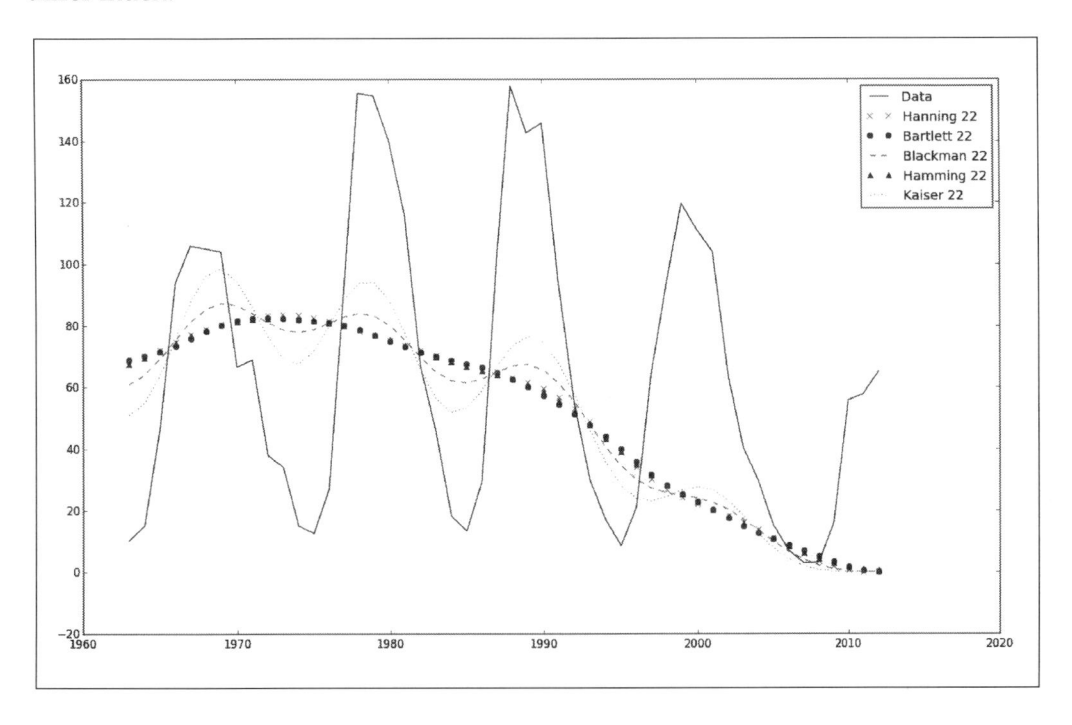

Forecasting with an ARMA model

In the previous chapter, *Chapter 4*, *Simple Predictive Analytics with NumPy*, we learned about autoregressive models. ARMA is a generalization of these models that adds an extra component—the moving average. ARMA models are frequently used to predict values of a time-series. These models combine autoregressive and moving-average models. Autoregressive models predict values by assuming that a linear combination is formed by the previously encountered values. For instance, we can consider a **linear combination**, which is formed from the previous value in the time-series and the value before that. This is also named an AR(2) model since we are using components that lag two periods. In our case, we would be looking at the number of sunspots one year before and two years before the period we are predicting. In an ARMA model, we try to model the residues that we cannot explain from the previous period data (also known as unexpected components). Here, a linear combination is assumed again. So an ARMA (ARMA (2, 1)) model, which we will attempt here is the sum of an AR(2) model and a linear combination of the first order residues (see http://en.wikipedia.org/wiki/Autoregressive%E2%80%93moving-average_model). Luckily, we can use the statsmodels functions for this analysis.

Signal Processing Techniques

We will also be using the sample sunspot data that is a part of the `statsmodels` distribution. This dataset might not be up to date depending on when you last installed `statsmodels`. In any case, you can always just use the dataset mentioned in the first section of this chapter. Forecasting can be done with the following steps:

1. Load the data in a `DataFrame` pandas. We also have to specify the available year ranges and get rid of the `Year` column using the following code:

   ```
   df = sm.datasets.sunspots.load_pandas().data

   df.index = pandas.Index(sm.tsa.datetools.dates_from_range('1700', '2008'))
   del df["YEAR"]
   ```

2. Fit the data to an ARMA(2,1) model using the following code:

   ```
   model = sm.tsa.ARMA(df, (2,1)).fit()
   ```

3. Do a forecast using the following code:

   ```
   prediction = model.predict('1984', str(year_today), dynamic=True)
   ```

The following code is the complete code listing with plotting:

```
import numpy as np
from scipy import stats
import pandas
import matplotlib.pyplot as plt
import statsmodels.api as sm
import datetime

df = sm.datasets.sunspots.load_pandas().data

df.index = pandas.Index(sm.tsa.datetools.dates_from_range('1700', '2008'))
del df["YEAR"]

model = sm.tsa.ARMA(df, (2,1)).fit()

year_today = datetime.date.today().year

#Big Brother is watching you!
prediction = model.predict('1984', str(year_today), dynamic=True)

df.plot()
prediction.plot(style='--', label='Prediction');
plt.legend();
plt.show()
```

[106]

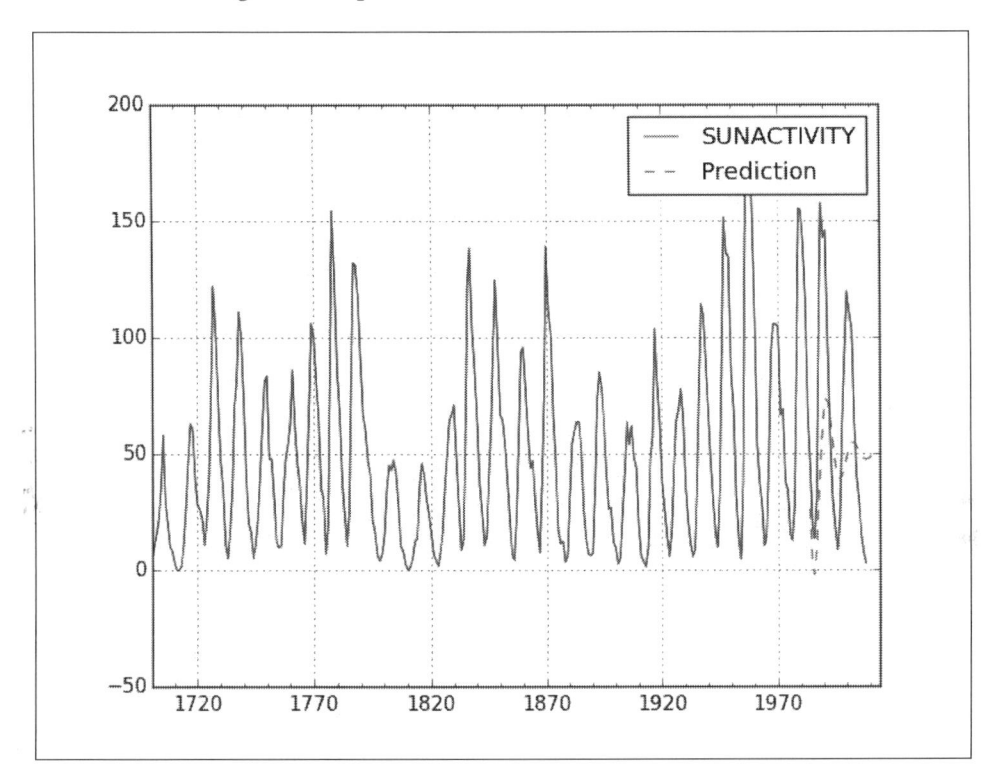

Refer to the following chart of prediction and actual data:

Filtering a signal

Another common signal processing technique is filtering. This is a big topic, and we could create all sorts of filters. We will only create a very basic filter here. Again, we will use the sunspot data as input.

The `iirdesign` function, as its name suggests, allows us to construct several types of analog and digital filters.

Designing the filter

Design the filter with the `iirdesign` function of the `scipy.signal` module.

> IIR stands for **Infinite Impulse Response**; for more information, visit http://en.wikipedia.org/wiki/Infinite_impulse_response.

We are not going to go into all the details of the `iirdesign` function. Have a look at the documentation if necessary at http://docs.scipy.org/doc/scipy/reference/generated/scipy.signal.iirdesign.html. In short, the following are the parameters we will set:

- Frequencies normalized from 0 to 1.
- Maximum loss.
- Minimum attenuation.
- Filter type.

Designing the filter can be done with the following code:

```
b,a = scipy.signal.iirdesign(wp=0.2, ws=0.1, gstop=60, gpass=1, ftype='but ter')
```

> The configuration of this filter corresponds to a Butterworth bandpass filter (http://en.wikipedia.org/wiki/Butterworth_filter).

We can apply the filter with the `scipy.signal.lfilter` function. It accepts as arguments the values from the previous step and, of course, the data array, to filter, as shown in the following code:

```
filtered = scipy.signal.lfilter(b, a, data)
```

If we plot the original data and the filtered data, we get the following plot:

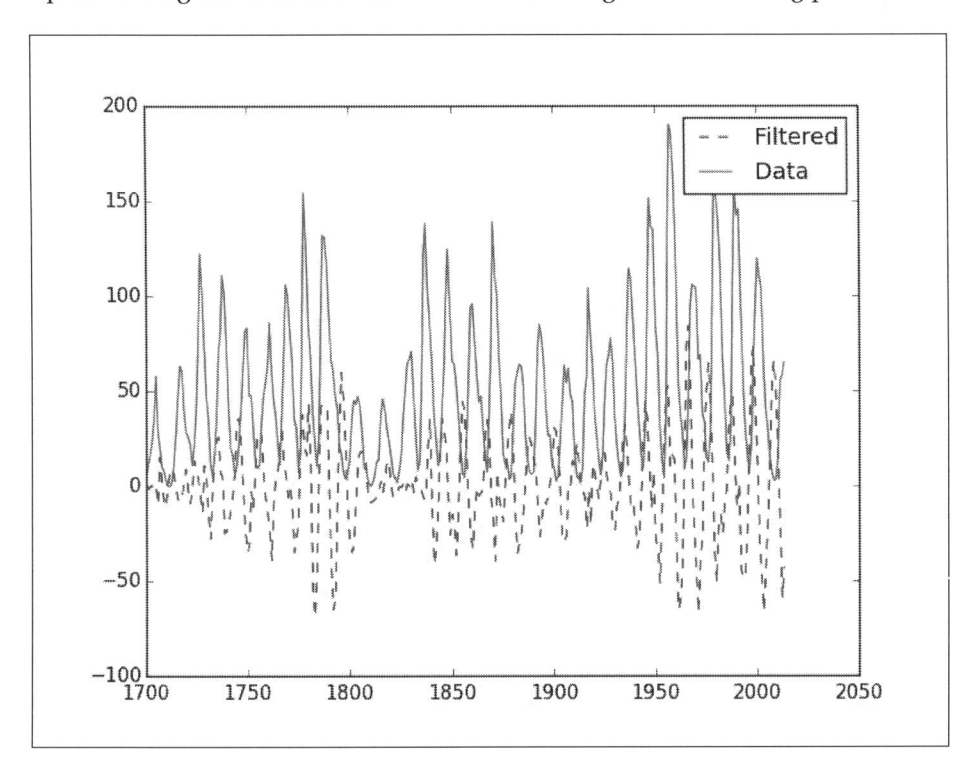

Demonstrating cointegration

Cointegration is similar to correlation, but it is considered by many to be a better metric to define the relatedness of two time-series. The usual way to explain the difference between cointegration and correlation is to take the example of a drunken man and his dog. Correlation tells you something about the direction in which they are going. Cointegration relates to their distance over time, which in this case is constrained by the leash of the dog. We will demonstrate cointegration using computer-generated time-series and real data. The data can be downloaded from Quandl in CSV format.

Signal Processing Techniques

The **Augmented Dickey Fuller (ADF)** test can be used to measure the cointegration of time-series; proceed with the following steps to demonstrate cointegration:

1. Define the following function to calculate the ADF statistic.

   ```
   def calc_adf(x, y):
       result = stat.OLS(x, y).fit()
       return ts.adfuller(result.resid)
   ```

2. Generate a `sine` value and calculate the cointegration of the value with itself:

   ```
   N = 501
   t = np.linspace(-2 * np.pi, 2 * np.pi, N)
   sine = np.sin(np.sin(t))
   print "Self ADF", calc_adf(sine, sine)
   ```

   This should print the following:

   Self ADF (2.9830728873654705e-17, 0.95853208606005602, 0, 500, {'5%': -2.8673378563200003, '1%': -3.4434963794639999, '10%': -2.5698580359999998}, -35895.784416878145)

   The first value you see is the ADF metric itself. The second number is the p-value. As you can observe, the p-value is quite high. Then follow the lag and sample size. The dictionary gives t-distribution values for this particular sample size.

3. Now add noise to the sine:

   ```
   noise = np.random.normal(0, .01, N)
   print "ADF sine with noise", calc_adf(sine, sine + noise)
   ```

   Adding noise gives the following results:

   ADF sine with noise (-23.84029624339999, 0.0, 0, 500, {'5%': -2.8673378563200003, '1%': -3.4434963794639999, '10%': -2.5698580359999998}, -3147.9631889288148)

   We can pretty much reject cointegration on the basis of the found p-value here it seems.

4. Let's generate a `cosine` value of a larger magnitude and offset. Again let's add the noise to it:

   ```
   cosine = 100 * np.cos(t) + 10
   print "ADF sine vs cosine with noise", calc_adf(sine, cosine + noise)
   ```

This gives the following values:

```
ADF sine vs cosine with noise (-4.7019725364090377,
8.3437700445205561e-05, 18, 482, {'5%': -2.8675550551408353,
'1%': -3.4439899743408136, '10%': -2.5699737921179042},
-18152.922572321968)
```

Again, here we see a strong rejection of cointegration.

5. Now on to real data that can be downloaded from URLs given in the following code snippet:

```
#http://www.quandl.com/BUNDESBANK/BBK01_WT5511-Gold-Price-USD
gold = np.loadtxt(sys.argv[1] + '/BBK01_WT5511.csv',
    delimiter=',', usecols=(1,), unpack=True, skiprows=1)


#http://www.quandl.com/YAHOO/INDEX_GSPC-S-P-500-Index
sp500 = np.loadtxt(sys.argv[1] + '/INDEX_GSPC.csv',
    delimiter=',', usecols=(6,), unpack=True, skiprows=1)
```

6. Here, we have to make sure that the two time-series are aligned and in the proper order:

```
sp500 = sp500[-len(gold):]
gold = gold[::-1]
sp500 = sp500[::-1]
print "Gold v S & P 500", calc_adf(gold, sp500)
```

The results show some evidence of cointegration it seems:

```
Gold v S & P 500 (-1.8835008669539355, 0.3398621844965054, 31,
11545, {'5%': -2.861790382593266, '1%': -3.4309165443532876,
'10%': -2.566903273565075}, 83668.547346270294)
```

Please refer to the following code:

```python
import numpy as np
import statsmodels.api as stat
import statsmodels.tsa.stattools as ts
import sys


def calc_adf(x, y):
    result = stat.OLS(x, y).fit()
    return ts.adfuller(result.resid)

N = 501
t = np.linspace(-2 * np.pi, 2 * np.pi, N)
sine = np.sin(np.sin(t))
```

```
print "Self ADF", calc_adf(sine, sine)

noise = np.random.normal(0, .01, N)
print "ADF sine with noise", calc_adf(sine, sine + noise)

cosine = 100 * np.cos(t) + 10
print "ADF sine vs cosine with noise", calc_adf(sine, cosine + noise)

#http://www.quandl.com/BUNDESBANK/BBK01_WT5511-Gold-Price-USD
gold = np.loadtxt(sys.argv[1] + '/BBK01_WT5511.csv', delimiter=',',
usecols=(1,), unpack=True, skiprows=1)

#http://www.quandl.com/YAHOO/INDEX_GSPC-S-P-500-Index
sp500 = np.loadtxt(sys.argv[1] + '/INDEX_GSPC.csv', delimiter=',',
usecols=(6,), unpack=True, skiprows=1)
sp500 = sp500[-len(gold):]
gold = gold[::-1]
sp500 = sp500[::-1]
print "Gold v S & P 500", calc_adf(gold, sp500)
```

Summary

In this chapter, we learned a number of sophisticated signal processing techniques. Most of them were applied to a dataset of sunspot data. We looked at smoothing with window functions and moving averages. We also touched upon the sifting process used by scientists to derive sunspot cycles. Last but not least, a demonstration was given of cointegration.

In the next chapter, we will focus on debugging, profiling, and testing, including assert functions and various tools.

6
Profiling, Debugging, and Testing

Profiling, debugging, and testing are an integral part of the development process. You are probably familiar with the concept of unit testing. Unit tests are automated tests written by a programmer to test his or her code. These tests could, for example, test a function or part of a function in isolation. Only a small unit of code is tested in each test. The benefits are increased confidence in the quality of the code, reproducible tests and, as a side effect, more clear and correct code. Unit testing also facilitates collaborative editing because, usually, no one understands all the code in a complex project themselves, so unit tests prevent contributors from breaking the existing code. Python has good support for unit testing. NumPy adds the `numpy.testing` package to help NumPy code the unit testing.

This chapter's topics include:

- Asserts
- Profiling
- Debugging
- Unit testing

Assert functions

The NumPy testing package has a number of utility functions that test whether a precondition is true or not. The following table lists the NumPy assert functions:

Function	Description
assert_almost_equal	This raises an exception if two numbers are not equal up to a specified precision
assert_approx_equal	This raises an exception if two numbers are not equal up to a certain significance
assert_array_almost_equal	This raises an exception if two arrays are not equal up to a specified precision
assert_array_equal	This raises an exception if two arrays are not equal
assert_array_less	This raises an exception if two arrays do not have the same shape, and the elements of the first array are strictly less than the elements of the second array
assert_equal	This raises an exception if two objects are not equal
assert_raises	This fails if a specified exception is not raised by a callable function invoked with defined arguments
assert_warns	This fails if a specified warning is not thrown
assert_string_equal	This asserts that two strings are equal

The assert_almost_equal function

Due to the nature of floating point numbers and the way they are represented by computers, we cannot always assert equality as we can for integers. Let's use the assert_almost_equal function to check whether they are equal:

1. Call the function with low precision (up to seven decimal places):

    ```
    print "Decimal 6", np.testing.assert_almost_equal(0.123456789,
    0.123456780, decimal=7)
    ```

    > Note that no exception is raised, as you can see in the following result:
    > Decimal 6 None

2. Call the function with high precision (up to eight decimal places):

    ```
    print "Decimal 7", np.testing.assert_almost_equal(0.123456789,
    0.123456780, decimal=8)
    ```

The result is:

```
Decimal 7
Traceback (most recent call last):
  ...
  raise AssertionError(msg)
AssertionError:
Arrays are not almost equal
 ACTUAL: 0.123456789
 DESIRED: 0.12345678
```

Approximately equal arrays

In this section, we will introduce another assert function. The `assert_approx_equal` function raises an exception if two numbers are not equal up to a certain number of significant digits. The function result is an exception that is triggered by the following condition:

```
abs(actual - expected) >= 10**-(significant - 1)
```

Let's take the numbers from the previous tutorial, and let the `assert_approx_equal` function work on them:

1. Call the function with low significance:

   ```
   print "Significance 8", np.testing.assert_approx_
   equal(0.123456789, 0.123456780,
   significant=8)
   ```

   The result is:

   Significance 8 None

2. Call the function with high significance:

   ```
   print "Significance 9",
     np.testing.assert_approx_equal
     (0.123456789, 0.123456780, significant=9)
   ```

   An exception is thrown:

   ```
   Significance 9
   Traceback (most recent call last):
   ...
     raise AssertionError(msg)
   ```

```
AssertionError:
Items are not equal to 9 significant digits:
 ACTUAL: 0.123456789
 DESIRED: 0.12345678
```

The assert_array_almost_equal function

Sometimes we need to check whether two arrays are almost equal. The `assert_array_almost_equal` function raises an exception if two arrays are not equal up to a specified precision. The function checks whether the two arrays have the same shape. Then, the values of the arrays are compared element by element as follows:

```
|expected - actual| < 0.5 10-decimal
```

Let's form arrays with the values from the previous tutorial by adding a zero to each array:

1. Calling the function with lower precision:

    ```
    print "Decimal 8", np.testing.assert_array_almost_equal([0,
       0.123456789], [0, 0.123456780], decimal=8)
    ```

    The result is:

    Decimal 8 None

2. Calling the function with higher precision:

    ```
    print "Decimal 9", np.testing.assert_array_almost_equal([0,
       0.123456789], [0, 0.123456780], decimal=9)
    ```

    An exception is thrown:

    ```
    Decimal 9
    Traceback (most recent call last):
      ...
     assert_array_compare
        raise AssertionError(msg)
    AssertionError:
    Arrays are not almost equal

    (mismatch 50.0%)
     x: array([ 0.        ,  0.12345679])
     y: array([ 0.        ,  0.12345678])
    ```

Profiling a program with IPython

As most of us learned in programming classes, premature optimization is the root of all evil. However, once you approach the final stages of software development, it could very well be that certain parts of the code are unnecessarily slow or use more memory than is strictly needed. We can find these issues through the process of profiling. Profiling involves measuring metrics such as execution time for a piece of code such as a function or a single statement.

IPython is an interactive Python environment, which also comes with a shell similar to the standard Python shell. In IPython, we can profile small snippets of code using `timeit`. We can also profile a larger script. We will show both approaches.

1. Timing a snippet:

    Start IPython in pylab mode

    ```
    ipython -pylab
    ```

2. Create an array containing 1,000 integer values between 0 and 1,000.

    ```
    In [1]: a = arange(1000)
    ```

    This is the time to search for the answer to everything 42 in the array.

    ```
    In [2]: %timeit searchsorted(a, 42)
    100000 loops, best of 3: 7.58 us per loop
    ```

3. Profile a script:

    We will profile this small script that inverts a matrix of varying size containing random values:

    ```
    import numpy

    def invert(n):
        a = numpy.matrix(numpy.random.rand(n, n))
        return a.I

    sizes = 2 ** numpy.arange(0, 12)
    ```

    for n in sizes:

    ```
        invert(n)
    ```

    We can time this as follows:

    ```
    In [1]: %run -t invert_matrix.py

    IPython CPU timings (estimated):
      User    :       6.08 s.
      System  :       0.52 s.
    Wall time:      19.26 s.
    ```

[117]

Then we can profile the script with the p option.

```
In [2]: %run -p invert_matrix.py


852 function calls in 6.597 CPU seconds

  Ordered by: internal time

    ncalls  tottime  percall  cumtime  percall filename:lineno(function)
        12    3.228    0.269    3.228    0.269 {numpy.linalg.lapack_lite.dgesv}
        24    2.967    0.124    2.967    0.124 {numpy.core.multiarray._fastCopyAndTranspose}
        12    0.156    0.013    0.156    0.013 {method 'rand' of 'mtrand.RandomState' objects}
        12    0.087    0.007    0.087    0.007 {method 'copy' of 'numpy.ndarray' objects}
        12    0.069    0.006    0.069    0.006 {method 'astype' of 'numpy.ndarray' objects}
        12    0.025    0.002    6.304    0.525 linalg.py:404(inv)
        12    0.024    0.002    6.328    0.527 defmatrix.py:808(getI)
         1    0.017    0.017    6.596    6.596 invert_matrix.py:1(<module>)
        24    0.014    0.001    0.014    0.001 {numpy.core.multiarray.zeros}
        12    0.009    0.001    6.580    0.548 invert_matrix.py:3(invert)
        12    0.000    0.000    6.264    0.522 linalg.py:244(solve)
        12    0.000    0.000    0.014    0.001 numeric.py:1875(identity)
         1    0.000    0.000    6.597    6.597 {execfile}
        36    0.000    0.000    0.000    0.000 defmatrix.py:279(__array_finalize__)
        12    0.000    0.000    2.967    0.247 linalg.py:139(_fastCopyAndTranspose)
```

```
        24    0.000    0.000    0.087    0.004 defmatrix.py:233(__
new__)
        12    0.000    0.000    0.000    0.000 linalg.py:99(_
commonType)
        24    0.000    0.000    0.000    0.000 {method '__array_
prepare__' of 'numpy.ndarray' objects}
        36    0.000    0.000    0.000    0.000 linalg.py:66(_
makearray)
        36    0.000    0.000    0.000    0.000 {numpy.core.
multiarray.array}
        12    0.000    0.000    0.000    0.000 {method 'view' of
'numpy.ndarray' objects}
        12    0.000    0.000    0.000    0.000 linalg.py:127(_to_
native_byte_order)
         1    0.000    0.000    6.597    6.597 interactiveshell.
py:2270(safe_execfile)
```

The interpretation for the column headers is the same as for the standard Python profiler (refer to `https://docs.python.org/2/library/profile.html#module-pstats`):

Header	Description
`ncalls`	This is the number of calls..
`tottime`	This is the total time spent in the given function (and excluding time spent in making calls to subfunctions).
`percall`	This is the quotient of `tottime` divided by `ncalls`.
`cumtime`	This is the total time spent in this and all subfunctions (from invocation till exit). This figure is accurate even for recursive functions.
`percall` (second)	This is the quotient of `cumtime` divided by primitive calls..

Debugging with IPython

Debugging is one of those tasks that we try to avoid by having good unit tests in place. Debugging can take a long time, and most likely, you don't have that time. Therefore, it is important to be systematic and know your tools well. After you have found the issue and implemented a fix, you should have a unit test in place. This way at least you will not have to go through the torture of debugging again.

Profiling, Debugging, and Testing

We will debug some incorrect code that is trying to access an array element out of bounds:

```
import numpy

a = numpy.arange(7)
print a[8]
```

Proceed with the following steps:

1. Run the faulty script in IPython.

    Start the `ipython` shell. Run the faulty script in IPython by issuing the following command:

    ```
    In [1]: %run buggy.py
    ---------------------------------------------------------------------------
    IndexError                                Traceback (most recent call last)
    .../site-packages/IPython/utils/py3compat.pyc in execfile(fname, *where)
        173             else:
        174                 filename = fname
    --> 175                 __builtin__.execfile(filename, *where)

    .../buggy.py in <module>()
          2
          3 a = numpy.arange(7)
    ----> 4 print a[8]


    IndexError: index out of bounds
    ```

2. Start the debugger.

    Now that our program crashed, we can start the debugger. This will set a breakpoint on the line where the error occurred:

    ```
    In [2]: %debug
    > .../buggy.py(4)<module>()
          2
          3 a = numpy.arange(7)
    ----> 4 print a[8]
    ```

[120]

3. List code.

   We can list code with the list command or use the shorthand l.

   ```
   ipdb> list
         1 import numpy
         2
         3 a = numpy.arange(7)
   ----> 4 print a[8]
   ```

4. Evaluate code at the current line.

   We can now evaluate arbitrary code at the current line.

   ```
   ipdb> len(a)
   7

   ipdb> print a
   [0 1 2 3 4 5 6]
   ```

5. View the call stack.

   We can view the call stack with the bt command:

   ```
   ipdb> bt
     .../py3compat.py(175)execfile()
         171              if isinstance(fname, unicode):
         172                  filename = fname.encode(sys.
   getfilesystemencoding())
         173              else:
         174                  filename = fname
   --> 175              __builtin__.execfile(filename, *where)

   > .../buggy.py(4)<module>()
         0 print a[8]
   ```

   Move the call stack up:

   ```
   ipdb> u
   > .../site-packages/IPython/utils/py3compat.py(175)execfile()
         173              else:
         174                  filename = fname
   --> 175              __builtin__.execfile(filename, *where)
   ```

[121]

Move the call stack down:

```
ipdb> d
> .../buggy.py(4)<module>()
      2
      3 a = numpy.arange(7)
----> 4 print a[8]
```

Performing Unit tests

Unit tests are automated tests that test a small piece of code, usually a function or method. Python has the PyUnit API for unit testing. As NumPy users, we can make use of the assert functions that we saw in action before.

We will write tests for a simple factorial function. The tests will check for the so-called happy path (regular conditions and is expected to always pass) and for abnormal conditions:

1. We start by writing the factorial function:

   ```
   def factorial(n):
      if n == 0:
         return 1

      if n < 0:
         raise ValueError, "Unexpected negative value"

      return np.arange(1, n+1).cumprod()
   ```

   The code is using the `arange` and `cumprod` functions that we have already seen to create arrays and calculate the cumulative product, but we added a few checks for boundary conditions.

2. Now we will write the unit test. Let's write a class that will contain the unit tests. It extends the `TestCase` class from the `unittest` module, which is a part of standard Python. We test for calling the factorial function with the following:
   - A positive number, the happy path
   - Boundary condition zero
   - Negative numbers, which should result in an error

```
class FactorialTest(unittest.TestCase):
   def test_factorial(self):
      #Test for the factorial of 3 that should pass.
      self.assertEqual(6, factorial(3)[-1])
      np.testing.assert_equal(np.array([1, 2, 6]), factorial(3))

   def test_zero(self):
      #Test for the factorial of 0 that should pass.
      self.assertEqual(1, factorial(0))

   def test_negative(self):
      #Test for the factorial of negative numbers that should fail.
      # It should throw a ValueError, but we expect IndexError
      self.assertRaises(IndexError, factorial(-10))
```

We rigged one of the tests to fail as you can see in the following output:

```
$ python unit_test.py
.E.
======================================================================
ERROR: test_negative (__main__.FactorialTest)
----------------------------------------------------------------------
Traceback (most recent call last):
  File "unit_test.py", line 26, in test_negative
    self.assertRaises(IndexError, factorial(-10))
  File "unit_test.py", line 9, in factorial
    raise ValueError, "Unexpected negative value"
ValueError: Unexpected negative value

----------------------------------------------------------------------
Ran 3 tests in 0.003s

FAILED (errors=1)
```

We made some happy path tests for the `factorial` function code. We let the boundary condition test fail on purpose (see `unit_test.py`) as follows:

```
import numpy as np
import unittest


def factorial(n):
    if n == 0:
        return 1

    if n < 0:
        raise ValueError, "Unexpected negative value"

    return np.arange(1, n+1).cumprod()


class FactorialTest(unittest.TestCase):
    def test_factorial(self):
        #Test for the factorial of 3 that should pass.
        self.assertEqual(6, factorial(3)[-1])
        np.testing.assert_equal(np.array([1, 2, 6]), factorial(3))

    def test_zero(self):
        #Test for the factorial of 0 that should pass.
        self.assertEqual(1, factorial(0))

    def test_negative(self):
        #Test for the factorial of negative numbers that should fail.
        # It should throw a ValueError, but we expect IndexError
        self.assertRaises(IndexError, factorial(-10))


if __name__ == '__main__':
    unittest.main()
```

Nose tests decorators

Nose is a Python framework that makes (unit) testing a bit easier. Nose helps you organize tests. According to the `nose` documentation:

> *Any python source file, directory or package that matches the testMatch regular expression (by default: (?:^|[b_.-])[Tt]est) will be collected as a test.*

Nose makes extensive use of decorators. Python decorators are annotations that indicate something about a method or a function. The `numpy.testing` module has a number of decorators:

Decorator	Description
`numpy.testing.decorators.deprecated`	This is the filter's deprecation warning when running tests
`numpy.testing.decorators.knownfailureif`	This raises the `KnownFailureTest` exception based on a condition.
`numpy.testing.decorators.setastest`	This marks a function as being a test or not being a test.
`numpy.testing.decorators.skipif`	This raises the `SkipTest` exception based on a condition.
`numpy.testing.decorators.slow`	This labels test functions or methods as slow.

Additionally, we can call the `decorate_methods` function to apply decorators on methods of a class matching a regular expression or a string.

We will apply the `setastest` decorator directly to test functions. Then we will apply the same decorator to a method to disable it. Also, we will skip one of the tests and fail another. First we will install `nose` as follows in the case that you don't have it yet:

1. Install `nose` with setup tools as follows:

   easy_install nose

   Or pip:

   pip install nose

2. Apply the decorators directly as follows:

   We will apply one function as being a test and another as not being a test:

   ```
   @setastest(False)
   def test_false():
   ```

```
    pass

@setastest(True)
def test_true():
    pass
```

3. Skip tests as follows:

   We can skip tests with the `skipif` decorator. Let's use a condition that always leads to a test being skipped:

   ```
   @skipif(True)
   def test_skip():
       pass
   ```

4. Fail tests with the `knownfailureif` decorator as follows:

   Add a test function that always passes. Then decorate it with the `knownfailureif` decorator so that the test always fails:

   ```
   @knownfailureif(True)
   def test_alwaysfail():
       pass
   ```

5. Define test classes as follows:

   We will define some test classes with methods that normally should be executed by nose:

   ```
   class TestClass():
       def test_true2(self):
           pass

   class TestClass2():
       def test_false2(self):
           pass
   ```

6. Disable a test method as follows:

   Let's disable the second test method from the previous step:

   ```
   decorate_methods(TestClass2, setastest(False), 'test_false2')
   ```

7. Run the tests as follows:

   We can run the tests with the following command:

   ```
   nosetests -v decorator_setastest.py
   decorator_setastest.TestClass.test_true2 ... ok
   ```

```
decorator_setastest.test_true ... ok
decorator_test.test_skip ... SKIP: Skipping test: test_skipTest
skipped due to test condition
decorator_test.test_alwaysfail ... ERROR


======================================================================
ERROR: decorator_test.test_alwaysfail
----------------------------------------------------------------------
Traceback (most recent call last):
  File "…/nose/case.py", line 197, in runTest
    self.test(*self.arg)
  File …/numpy/testing/decorators.py", line 213, in knownfailer
    raise KnownFailureTest(msg)
KnownFailureTest: Test skipped due to known failure

----------------------------------------------------------------------
Ran 4 tests in 0.001s

FAILED (SKIP=1, errors=1)
```

8. We decorated some functions and methods as not being tests so that they were ignored by nose. We skipped one test and failed another too. We did this by applying decorators directly and with the following `decorate_methods` function (see `decorator_test.py`):

```
from numpy.testing.decorators import setastest
from numpy.testing.decorators import skipif
from numpy.testing.decorators import knownfailureif
from numpy.testing import decorate_methods


@setastest(False)
def test_false():
    pass

@setastest(True)
def test_true():
```

```python
    pass

@skipif(True)
def test_skip():
    pass

@knownfailureif(True)
def test_alwaysfail():
    pass


class TestClass():
    def test_true2(self):
        pass


class TestClass2():
    def test_false2(self):
        pass


decorate_methods(TestClass2, setastest(False), 'test_false2')
```

Summary

We learned about testing and NumPy testing utilities in this chapter. We covered unit testing, assert functions, profiling, and debugging. Unit testing is a standard practice since it should give you better quality code with a low risk of regression. NumPy provides assert functions to help you with unit testing. We covered some of these functions in this chapter. No matter how good your unit tests are, at a certain point, you will have to do profiling and debugging, so pointers are given in that respect.

The topic of the next chapter is the scientific Python ecosystem and how NumPy fits in it.

7
The Scientific Python Ecosystem

SciPy is built on top of NumPy. It adds functionality such as numerical integration, optimization, statistics, and special functions. Historically, NumPy was part of SciPy but was then separated in order to be used by other Python libraries. These, when combined, define the common stack for scientific and numerical analysis. Of course, the stack itself is not set in stone; however, everybody agrees on NumPy being at the center of it all. The examples in this chapter should give you some idea about the power of the scientific Python ecosystem.

In this chapter, we will cover the following topics:

- Numerical integration
- Interpolation
- Using Cython with NumPy
- Clustering with scikit-learn
- Detecting corners
- Comparing NumPy to Blaze

Numerical integration

Numerical integration is integration using numerical methods instead of analytical methods. SciPy has a numerical integration package, `scipy.integrate`, which has no equivalent in NumPy. The `quad` function can integrate a one-variable function between two points. These points can be at infinity.

> The `quad` function uses the old and tried QUADPACK Fortran library under the hood.

The Gaussian integral is related to the `error` function, but has no finite limits. It evaluates to the square root of *pi*. Let's calculate the Gaussian integral with the `quad` function as shown in the following line of code:

```
print "Gaussian integral", np.sqrt(np.pi),
integrate.quad(lambda x: np.exp(-x**2),
-np.inf, np.inf)
```

The return value is the outcome, and its error would be:

```
Gaussian integral 1.77245385091 (1.7724538509055159,
  1.4202636780944923e-08)
```

Interpolation

Interpolation predicts values within a range based on observations. For instance, we could have a relationship between two variables x and y and we have a set of observed x-y pairs. In this scenario, we could try to predict the y value given a range of x values. This range will start at the lowest x value already observed and end at the highest x value already observed. The `scipy.interpolate` function interpolates a function based on experimental data. The `interp1d` class can create a linear or cubic interpolation function. By default, a linear interpolation function is constructed, but if the `kind` parameter is set, a cubic interpolation function is created instead. The `interp2d` class works in the same way but is two dimensional.

We will create data points using a `sinc` function and then add some random noise to it. After that, we will do a linear and cubic interpolation and plot the results as follows:

1. Create the data points and add noise as follows:
   ```
   x = np.linspace(-18, 18, 36)
   noise = 0.1 * np.random.random(len(x))
   signal = np.sinc(x) + noise
   ```

2. Create a linear interpolation function, and then apply it to an input array with five times as many data points:
   ```
   interpolated = interpolate.interp1d(x, signal)
   x2 = np.linspace(-18, 18, 180)
   y = interpolated(x2)
   ```

3. Do the same as in the previous step but with cubic interpolation:
   ```
   cubic = interpolate.interp1d(x, signal, kind="cubic")
   y2 = cubic(x2)
   ```

4. Plot the results with Matplotlib as follows:

   ```
   plt.plot(x, signal, 'o', label="data")
   plt.plot(x2, y, '-', label="linear")
   plt.plot(x2, y2, '--', lw=2, label="cubic")

   plt.legend()
   plt.show()
   ```

   The following diagram is a plot of the data, linear, and cubic interpolations:

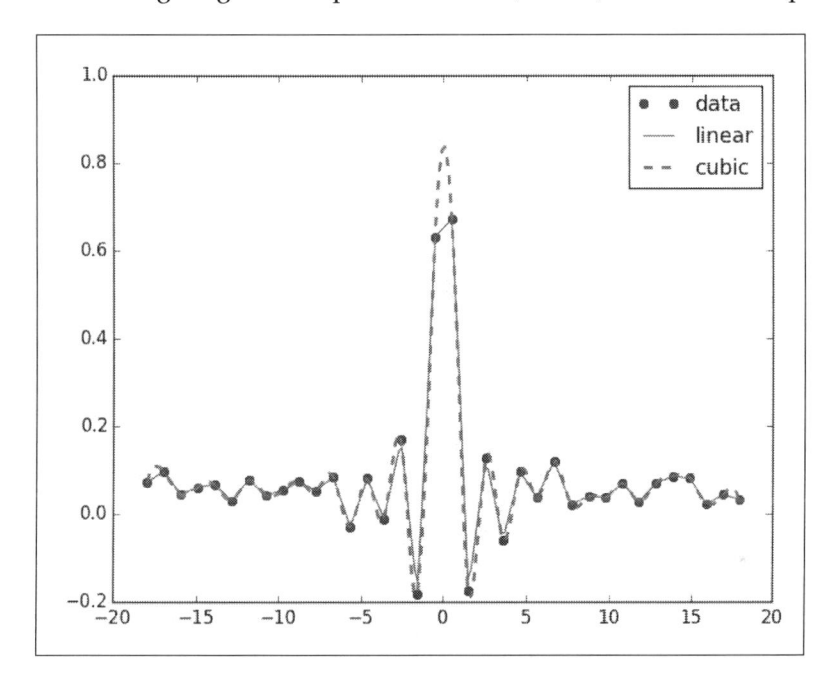

We created a dataset from the `sinc` function and added noise to it. We then did linear and cubic interpolation using the `interp1d` class of the `scipy.interpolate` module (see the `sincinterp.py` file in the `Chapter07` folder of this book's code bundle):

```
import numpy as np
from scipy import interpolate
import matplotlib.pyplot as plt

x = np.linspace(-18, 18, 36)
noise = 0.1 * np.random.random(len(x))
signal = np.sinc(x) + noise

interpolated = interpolate.interp1d(x, signal)
x2 = np.linspace(-18, 18, 180)
```

```
y = interpolated(x2)

cubic = interpolate.interp1d(x, signal, kind="cubic")
y2 = cubic(x2)

plt.plot(x, signal, 'o', label="data")
plt.plot(x2, y, '-', label="linear")
plt.plot(x2, y2, '--', lw=2, label="cubic")

plt.legend()
plt.show()
```

Using Cython with NumPy

Cython is a relatively young programming language based on Python. The difference is that with Python we can optionally declare static types for variables in the code. Cython is a compiled language that generates CPython extension modules. Besides providing performance enhancement, a major use of Cython is interfacing already existing C/C++ software with Python.

We can integrate Cython and NumPy code in the same way that we can integrate Cython and Python code. Let's go through an example that analyses the ratio of up days (close higher than the previous day) for a stock. We will apply the formula for binomial proportion confidence (http://en.wikipedia.org/wiki/Binomial_proportion_confidence_interval). This indicates how significant the ratio is.

1. Write a .pyx file.

   The .pyx files contain Cython code. Basically, Cython code is standard Python code with optional static type declarations added for variables. Let's write a .pyx file that contains a function that calculates the ratio of up days and their associated confidence. Firstly, this function computes the differences between the prices. Then, we count the number of positive differences, giving us a ratio for the proportion of up days. Finally, we apply the formula for the confidence from the Wikipedia page in the introduction, as follows.

   ```
   import numpy

   def pos_confidence(numbers):
       diffs = numpy.diff(numbers)
       n = float(len(diffs))
       p = len(diffs[diffs > 0])/n
       confidence = numpy.sqrt(p * (1 - p)/ n)

       return (p, confidence)
   ```

2. Write the `setup.py` file.

   We will use the following `setup.py` file:

   ```
   from distutils.core import setup
   from distutils.extension import Extension
   from Cython.Distutils import build_ext

   ext_modules = [Extension("binomial_proportion",
     ["binomial_proportion.pyx"])]

   setup(
           name = 'Binomial proportion app',
           cmdclass = {'build_ext': build_ext},
           ext_modules = ext_modules
         )
   ```

3. Now, use the Cython module.

   We can build with the following command:

   python setup.py build_ext --inplace

   After building, we can use the Cython module from the previous step by importing. We will write a Python program that downloads stock price data with Matplotlib. Then, we will apply the confidence function to the close prices.

   ```
   from matplotlib.finance import quotes_historical_yahoo
   from datetime import date
   import numpy
   import sys
   from binomial_proportion import pos_confidence

   #1. Get close prices.
   today = date.today()
   start = (today.year - 1, today.month, today.day)

   quotes = quotes_historical_yahoo(sys.argv[1], start, today)
   close =  numpy.array([q[4] for q in quotes])
   print pos_confidence(close)
   ```

   The output of the program for AAPL is as follows:

   `(0.56746031746031744, 0.031209043355655924)`

The Scientific Python Ecosystem

Clustering stocks with scikit-learn

Scikit-learn is an open source software for machine learning. Clustering is a type of machine learning algorithm that aims to group items based on similarities.

> A legion of scikits exists. These are all open source scientific Python projects. For a list of scikits, please refer to https://scikits.appspot.com/scikits.

Clustering is unsupervised, which means that you don't have to create learning examples. The algorithm puts items in the appropriate bucket based on some measure of distance, so that items that are close to each other end up in the same bucket. In this example, we will use the log returns of stocks in the **Dow Jones Industrial (DJI)** Index to cluster.

> A myriad of clustering algorithms exist, and since this is a rapidly evolving field, new algorithms are invented each year. Due to the exigencies of this book, we cannot touch upon all of them. The interested reader can have a look at https://en.wikipedia.org/wiki/Cluster_analysis.

First, we will download EOD price data for these stocks from Yahoo Finance. Second, we will calculate a square affinity matrix. Finally, we will cluster the stocks with the `AffinityPropagation` class. Affinity propagation, in contrast to other clustering algorithms, doesn't require the number of clusters as a parameter. The algorithm relies on a so-called affinity matrix. This is a matrix that contains affinities of data points, which can be interpreted as distances.

1. We will download price data for 2013 using the stock symbols of the DJI Index. In this example, we are only interested in the close price. The code is as follows:

    ```
    # 2012 to 2013
    start = datetime.datetime(2012, 01, 01)
    end = datetime.datetime(2013, 01, 01)

    #Dow Jones symbols
    symbols = ["AA", "AXP", "BA", "BAC", "CAT",
       "CSCO", "CVX", "DD", "DIS", "GE", "HD",
       "HPQ", "IBM", "INTC", "JNJ", "JPM",
       "KO", "MCD", "MMM", "MRK", "MSFT", "PFE",
       "PG", "T", "TRV", "UTX", "VZ", "WMT", "XOM"]

    for symbol in symbols:
        try :
    ```

```
            quotes.append(finance.quotes_historical_yahoo_
ochl(symbol,
   start, end, asobject=True))
         except urllib2.HTTPError:
            print symbol, "not found"

close = np.array([q.close for q in
   quotes]).astype(np.float)
```

2. Calculate the similarities between different stocks using the log returns as the metric. The code is as follows:

```
logreturns = np.diff(np.log(close))
print logreturns.shape

logreturns_norms = np.sum(logreturns ** 2, axis=1)
S = - logreturns_norms[:, np.newaxis] -
   logreturns_norms[np.newaxis, :] + 2 * np.dot(logreturns,
   logreturns.T)
```

3. Give the `AffinityPropagation` class the result from the previous step. This class labels the data points or, in our case, stocks, with the appropriate cluster number. The code is as follows:

```
aff_pro = sklearn.cluster.AffinityPropagation().fit(S)
labels = aff_pro.labels_

for i in xrange(len(labels)):
    print '%s in Cluster %d' % (symbols[i], labels[i])
```

The following is the complete clustering program:

```
import datetime
import numpy as np
import sklearn.cluster
from matplotlib import finance
import urllib2

#1. Download price data

# 2012 to 2013
start = datetime.datetime(2012, 01, 01)
end = datetime.datetime(2013, 01, 01)

#Dow Jones symbols
```

```
symbols = ["AA", "AXP", "BA", "BAC", "CAT",
  "CSCO", "CVX", "DD", "DIS", "GE", "HD",
  "HPQ", "IBM", "INTC", "JNJ", "JPM",
  "KO", "MCD", "MMM", "MRK", "MSFT", "PFE",
  "PG", "T", "TRV", "UTX", "VZ", "WMT", "XOM"]

quotes = []
```

For symbols within symbols, the code is as follows:

```
    try :
quotes.append(finance.quotes_historical_yahoo_ochl(symbol,
    start, end, asobject=True))
    except urllib2.HTTPError:
        print symbol, "not found"

close = np.array([q.close for q in quotes]).astype(np.float)
print close.shape

#2. Calculate affinity matrix
logreturns = np.diff(np.log(close))
print logreturns.shape

logreturns_norms = np.sum(logreturns ** 2, axis=1)
S = - logreturns_norms[:, np.newaxis] -
    logreturns_norms[np.newaxis, :] + 2 * np.dot(logreturns,
    logreturns.T)

#3. Cluster using affinity propagation
aff_pro = sklearn.cluster.AffinityPropagation().fit(S)
labels = aff_pro.labels_

for i in xrange(len(labels)):
    print '%s in Cluster %d' % (symbols[i], labels[i])
```

The output with the cluster numbers for each stock is as follows:

AA in Cluster 2

AXP in Cluster 0

BA in Cluster 0

BAC in Cluster 1

CAT in Cluster 2

CSCO in Cluster 3

CVX in Cluster 8

DD in Cluster 0

```
DIS in Cluster 6
GE in Cluster 8
HD in Cluster 0
HPQ in Cluster 4
IBM in Cluster 0
INTC in Cluster 0
JNJ in Cluster 6
JPM in Cluster 5
KO in Cluster 6
MCD in Cluster 6
MMM in Cluster 8
MRK in Cluster 6
MSFT in Cluster 0
PFE in Cluster 6
PG in Cluster 6
T in Cluster 6
TRV in Cluster 6
UTX in Cluster 0
VZ in Cluster 6
WMT in Cluster 7
XOM in Cluster 8
```

Detecting corners

Corner detection is a standard technique in computer vision. Scikits-image (a package specialized in image processing) offers a Harris corner detector, which is great since corner detection is pretty complicated. Obviously, we could do it ourselves from scratch, but that would violate the cardinal rule of not reinventing the wheel. We will load a sample image from scikits-learn. This is not absolutely necessary for this example. You can use any other image instead.

> For more information on corner detection, please refer to https://en.wikipedia.org/wiki/Corner_detection.

The Scientific Python Ecosystem

You might need to install jpeglib on your system to be able to load the scikits-learn image, which is a JPEG file. If you are on Windows, use the installer; otherwise, download the distribution, unpack it, and build from the top folder with the following command line:

```
./configure
 make
  sudo make install
```

To detect corners of an image, perform the following steps:

1. Load the sample image.

   Scikits-learn currently has two sample JPEG images in a dataset structure. We will look at the first image only, as follows:
   ```
   dataset = load_sample_images()
   img = dataset.images[0]
   ```

2. Then, detect corners by calling the `harris` function to get the coordinates of corners:
   ```
   harris_coords = harris(img)
   print "Harris coords shape", harris_coords.shape
   y, x = np.transpose(harris_coords)
   ```

   The code for corner detection is given as follows:
   ```
   from sklearn.datasets import load_sample_images
   from matplotlib.pyplot import imshow, show, axis, plot
   import numpy as np
   from skimage.feature import harris

   dataset = load_sample_images()
   img = dataset.images[0]
   harris_coords = harris(img)
   print "Harris coords shape", harris_coords.shape
   y, x = np.transpose(harris_coords)
   axis('off')
   imshow(img)
   plot(x, y, 'ro')
   show()
   ```

We get an image with red dots, where corners are detected as follows:

Comparing NumPy to Blaze

Since we are close to the end of the book, it seems appropriate to discuss the future of NumPy. The future of NumPy is Blaze, a new open source Python numerical library. Blaze is supposed to process Big Data better than NumPy ever can. Big Data can be defined in many ways. Here, we will define Big Data as data that cannot be stored in memory or even on a single machine. Usually, the data is distributed amongst several servers. Blaze should also be able to handle large quantities of streaming data that is never stored.

> Blaze can be found at http://blaze.pydata.org/.

Blaze, just like NumPy, allows scientists, analysts, and engineers to quickly write efficient code. Blaze, however, goes a step further and also takes care of the work related to distributing calculations as well as extracting and transforming data from a variety of data source types.

Blaze is centered around general multidimensional array and table abstractions. The classes in Blaze represent different data types and data structures as found in the real world. Blaze has a generic computation engine that can process data spread out over multiple servers and send instructions to specialized low-level kernels.

Blaze extends NumPy to provide custom-defined data types and heterogeneous shapes. This, of course, allows for greater flexibility and ease of use.

Blaze is designed around arrays. Just like the NumPy `ndarray`, Blaze offers metadata with extra computational information. The metadata defines how data is stored, (heterogeneously) typed and indexed as multidimensional arrays. Computation can be performed on various hardware including heterogeneous clusters of CPUs and GPUs.

Blaze has the ambition to become the NumPy of multiple node clusters and distributed computing. The main idea, just as with NumPy, is to focus on arrays and array operations while abstracting the messy details away.

> Blaze has a special LLVM compiler. For more information about the LLVM compiler, see `http://en.wikipedia.org/wiki/LLVM`. In short, LLVM is an open source compiler technology project.

Data can be converted between different formats using the Blaze data adapters. Blaze also manages scheduling of computations, which can be either automatic or configured by the user, with the possibility to lazily evaluate expressions.

Summary

In this chapter, we only scratched the surface of what is possible with the scientific Python ecosystem. We used some of the libraries that are considered, if not part of the common stack, then at least fundamental. We used interpolation and numerical integration provided by SciPy. Two of the dozens of algorithms in scikit-learn were demonstrated. We also saw Cython in action, which is technically a programming language in its own right. Finally, we had a look at Blaze, a library supposed to generalize and extend the principles of NumPy. This is in light of recent developments such as Big Data and Cloud Computing. Blaze and related projects are still in the incubation phase, but we can expect stable software to be produced in the near future. You can refer to `http://continuum.io/developer-resources` for some of these projects.

Unfortunately, we have come to the end of this book. Because of this book's format, that is the number of pages, you should have essential NumPy knowledge and might feel the need for more. However, don't worry if this wasn't enough for you. You can look forward to *Learning Python Data Analysis* by the same author, which will come out in early 2015.

Index

Symbols

#scipy channel 18

A

adjusted autoregressive model
 setting up 89, 90
ARMA model
 about 105
 used, for forecasting 105, 106
array() function 21
array shapes, NumPy
 array attributes 35
 arrays, converting 38
 arrays, flattening 28
 arrays, splitting 33
 arrays, stacking 29
 manipulating 28
assert_almost_equal function 114
assert_approx_equal function 114, 115
assert_array_almost_equal function 114, 116
assert_array_equal function 114
assert_array_less function 114
assert_equal function 114
assert functions, NumPy
 about 114
 assert_almost_equal function 114
 assert_approx_equal function 115, 116
 assert_array_almost_equal function 116
assert_raises function 114
assert_string_equal function 114
assert_warns function 114
atmospheric humidity 69
atmospheric humidity, KNMI De Bilt
  data file
 analyzing 69-71

atmospheric pressure 67
atmospheric pressure, KNMI De Bilt
  data file
 analyzing 67-69
Augmented Dickey Fuller (ADF) test 110
Autoregressive (AR) model 88
Autoregressive Moving Average (ARMA)
  model 88
average De Bilt temperature
 outliers analysis 92
average temperature autocorrelation
 examining, with pandas 73-76

B

basic data analysis
 dataset 51
Blaze
 about 139
 NumPy, comparing with 139
 URL 139
Boolean indexing
 about 43
 performing 43, 44

C

character codes 24
clustering 134
cointegration
 about 109
 demonstrating 109-111
column_stack() function 31
column stacking, NumPy arrays 31
concatenate() function 30
corner detection
 about 137

performing 138
Cython
 about 132
 using, with NumPy 132, 133

D

daily temperature range, KNMI De Bilt data file
 about 53
 determining 53, 54
data analysis, KNMI weather station
 daily temperature range, determining 53, 54
 De Bilt atmospheric humidity, analyzing 69-71
 De Bilt atmospheric pressure, analyzing 67, 68
 De Bilt precipitation data, analyzing 66, 67
 precipitation, analyzing 63-66
 solar radiation, comparing with temperature 57-59
 sunshine duration, analyzing 63-66
 wind direction, analyzing 61
 wind speed, analyzing 62, 63
 yearly average temperature, determining 55, 56
data type objects 24
day-of-the-year temperature model
 about 83
 used, for modeling temperature 85
debugging
 about 119
 IPython, used 119, 120
decorators
 applying 125-127
deprecated decorator 125
depth stacking, NumPy arrays 31
depth-wise splitting, NumPy arrays 34
Dow Jones Industrial (DJI) 134
dsplit() function 34
dtype attributes 26
dtype constructors 25

E

Empirical Mode Decomposition (EMD) 97

F

fancy indexing
 about 40
 performing 40, 41
filter
 designing 108
flat attribute, ndarray 37
flatten() function 28
forecasting
 ARMA model, used 105, 106

G

Gaussian integral 130

H

horizontal splitting, NumPy arrays 33
horizontal stacking, NumPy arrays 29

I

iirdesign function 107
imag attribute, ndarray 36
interp1d class 130
interpolation 130, 131
inter-quartile range 92
intra-year daily average temperatures
 analyzing 81, 82
Intrinsic Mode Functions (IMF)
 about 97
 extracting, via sifting 98
IPython
 about 117
 debugging with 119, 121
 installing, on Linux 10
 installing, on Windows 8, 9
 program, profiling with 117, 118
itemsize attribute, ndarray 35
ix_() function 42

K

KNMI
 about 51
 URL 51
knownfailureif decorator 125

L

linear combination 105
Linux
  IPython, installing 10
  Matplotlib, installing 10
  NumPy, installing 10
  SciPy, installing 10
Linux distributions
  Arch Linux 10
  Debian 10
  Fedora 10
  Gentoo 10
  OpenSUSE 10
  Slackware 10
loadtxt function 52

M

Mac OS X
  Matplotlib, installing 12, 13
  NumPy, installing 11, 12
  SciPy, installing 13
Matplotlib
  installing, on Linux 10
  installing, on Mac OS X 13
  installing, on Windows 9
monthly precipitation, KNMI De Bilt data file
  analyzing 66, 67
Moving Average (MA) model 88
moving averages
  about 101
  plotting 102
moving average temperature model 87
multidimensional NumPy array
  creating 21

N

nbytes attribute, ndarray 35
ndarray
  about 19
  flat attribute 37
  imag attribute 36
  itemsize attribute 35
  nbytes attribute 35
  ndim attribute 35

  real attribute 36
  size attribute 35
  T attribute 36
ndim attribute, ndarray 35
nose
  about 125
  decorators, using 125
  installing 125
Not a Number (NaN) 52
numerical integration 129, 130
NumPy
  about 7
  assert functions 114
  basic data analysis 51
  building, from source 14
  comparing, to Blaze 139, 140
  Cython, using with 132, 133
  forum link 18
  installing, on Linux 10
  installing, on Mac OS X 11
  installing, on Windows 8, 9
  online resources 18
  predictive analytics 73
NumPy array object 19
NumPy arrays
  about 14
  adding 15, 17
  advantages 20
  array elements, selecting 21, 22
  broadcasting 47, 48
  converting 38
  fancy indexing 40
  indexing, performing with list of locations 42, 43
  indexing, with Booleans 43, 44
  one-dimensional, indexing 27
  one-dimensional, slicing 27
  record data type, creating 26
  stride tricks, applying for Sudoku 45, 47
  views, creating 39, 40
NumPy basics
  NumPy array object 19
NumPy numerical types
  bool 22
  character codes 24
  complex 23
  complex64 23

complex128 23
data type objects 24
dtype attributes 26
dtype constructors 25
float16 22
float32 22
float64 22
int8 22
int16 22
int32 22
int64 22
inti 22
overview 22, 23
uint8 22
uint16 22
uint32 22
uint64 22
numpy.testing module
  decorators 125

O

one-dimensional NumPy arrays
  indexing 27
  slicing 27
outliers analysis, average De Bilt
    temperature
  performing 92, 93

P

pandas DataFrame
  used, for descriptive statistics 76
pandas library
  about 73
  used, for correlating weather and stocks 78
  used, for examining average temperature autocorrelation 73-76
precipitation, KNMI De Bilt data file
  analyzing 63-66
predictive analytics
  average temperature autocorrelation, examining with pandas 73-76
  data, describing with pandas DataFrames 76
  day-of-the-year temperature 85

day-of-the-year temperature model 83
intra-year daily average temperatures, analyzing 81, 82
moving average temperature model 87
temperature, modeling with SciPy leastsq function 84
temperature, predicting 79
weather and stocks, correlating with pandas 78
program
  profiling, with IPython 117, 118
Python 7
PyUnit API 122

Q

quad function 129

R

ravel() function 28
real attribute, ndarray 36
record data type
  about 26
  creating 26
resize() method 29
robust statistics 94
row stacking, NumPy arrays 32

S

scikit-learn
  about 134
  used, for clustering stocks 134-136
SciPy
  about 7, 129
  forum link 18
  installing, on Linux 10
  installing, on Mac OS X 11-13
  installing, on Windows 9
  online resources 18
scipy.integrate 129
scipy.interpolate function 130
SciPy leastsq function
  used, for modeling temperature 84
setastest decorator 125

[144]

shape() function 28
sifting process
  about 98
  steps 99-101
signal
  filtering 107
signal processing techniques
  about 97
  moving averages 101
  Sunspot data 97
size attribute, ndarray 35
skipif decorator 125
slow decorator 125
smoothing functions 103, 104
solar radiation
  comparing, with temperature 57-59
split() function 33
splitting, NumPy arrays
  depth-wise splitting 34
  horizontal splitting 33
  performing 33
  vertical splitting 34
stacking, NumPy arrays
  column stacking 31
  depth stacking 31
  horizontal stacking 29
  performing 29
  row stacking 32
  vertical stacking 30
stocks
  clustering, with scikit-learn 134-136
stride tricks
  applying, to Sudoku 45, 46
sunshine duration, KNMI De Bilt data file
  analyzing 63-66
sunspot data 97, 98
sunspots 97

T

T attribute, ndarray 36

temperature
  autoregressive model with lag 1 79
  autoregressive model with lag 2 80
  modeling, with SciPy leastsq function 84
  predicting 79
transpose() function 29

U

unit tests
  performing 122, 124

V

vertical splitting, NumPy arrays 34
vertical stacking, NumPy arrays 30
views, NumPy arrays
  creating 39, 40
vsplit() function 34

W

weather and stocks
  correlating, with pandas 78
wind direction, KNMI De Bilt data file
  analyzing 61
Windows
  IPython, installing 8
  Matplotlib, installing 9
  NumPy, installing 8, 9
  SciPy, installing 9
wind speed, KNMI De Bilt data file
  analyzing 62

Y

yearly average temperature, KNMI De Bilt data file
  determining 55, 56

[PACKT] open source
PUBLISHING — community experience distilled

Thank you for buying
Learning NumPy Array

About Packt Publishing

Packt, pronounced 'packed', published its first book "*Mastering phpMyAdmin for Effective MySQL Management*" in April 2004 and subsequently continued to specialize in publishing highly focused books on specific technologies and solutions.

Our books and publications share the experiences of your fellow IT professionals in adapting and customizing today's systems, applications, and frameworks. Our solution based books give you the knowledge and power to customize the software and technologies you're using to get the job done. Packt books are more specific and less general than the IT books you have seen in the past. Our unique business model allows us to bring you more focused information, giving you more of what you need to know, and less of what you don't.

Packt is a modern, yet unique publishing company, which focuses on producing quality, cutting-edge books for communities of developers, administrators, and newbies alike. For more information, please visit our website: www.packtpub.com.

About Packt Open Source

In 2010, Packt launched two new brands, Packt Open Source and Packt Enterprise, in order to continue its focus on specialization. This book is part of the Packt Open Source brand, home to books published on software built around Open Source licenses, and offering information to anybody from advanced developers to budding web designers. The Open Source brand also runs Packt's Open Source Royalty Scheme, by which Packt gives a royalty to each Open Source project about whose software a book is sold.

Writing for Packt

We welcome all inquiries from people who are interested in authoring. Book proposals should be sent to author@packtpub.com. If your book idea is still at an early stage and you would like to discuss it first before writing a formal book proposal, contact us; one of our commissioning editors will get in touch with you.

We're not just looking for published authors; if you have strong technical skills but no writing experience, our experienced editors can help you develop a writing career, or simply get some additional reward for your expertise.

[PACKT] open source*
PUBLISHING
community experience distilled

NumPy Beginner's Guide
Second Edition

ISBN: 978-1-78216-608-5 Paperback: 310 pages

An action packed guide using real world examples of the easy to use, high performance, free open source NumPy mathematical library

1. Perform high performance calculations with clean and efficient NumPy code.
2. Analyze large data sets with statistical functions.
3. Execute complex linear algebra and mathematical computations.

NumPy Cookbook

ISBN: 978-1-84951-892-5 Paperback: 226 pages

Over 70 interesting recipes for learning the Python open source mathematical library, NumPy

1. Do high performance calculations with clean and efficient NumPy code.
2. Analyze large sets of data with statistical functions.
3. Execute complex linear algebra and mathematical computations.

Please check www.PacktPub.com for information on our titles

[PACKT] open source*
PUBLISHING   community experience distilled

Learning IPython for Interactive Computing and Data Visualization

ISBN: 978-1-78216-993-2   Paperback: 138 pages

Learn IPython for interactive Python programming, high-performance numerical computing, and data visualization

1. A practical step-by-step tutorial which will help you to replace the Python console with the powerful IPython command-line interface.

2. Use the IPython notebook to modernize the way you interact with Python.

3. Perform highly efficient computations with NumPy and Pandas.

Learning SciPy for Numerical and Scientific Computing

ISBN: 978-1-78216-162-2   Paperback: 150 pages

A practical tutorial that guarantees fast, accurate, and easy-to-code solutions to your numerical and scientific computing problems with the power of SciPy and Python

1. Perform complex operations with large matrices, including eigenvalue problems, matrix decompositions, or solution to large systems of equations.

2. Step-by-step examples to easily implement statistical analysis and data mining that rivals in performance any of the costly specialized software suites.

Please check **www.PacktPub.com** for information on our titles

Made in the USA
Columbia, SC
08 December 2024